GETTING THE BENEFITS YOU HAVE EARNED PART 2

Explaining the Unexplained about VETERAN BENEFITS

by

Tammy James

Written by Tammy James
Self-Published by Tammy James

(A Veteran helping another Veterans)

Dedication:

To the Love of my Life and Kids for always giving me that motivation to succeed, you mean the world to me and will always be in my heart.

To my awesome sister Tekecia (Kiki) aka my Mother. Thanks for all you have done and continue to do. You have made me the person I am today. When I thought, I couldn't you always believed in me. You pushed me to be great. Thanks Sis and I love you for keeping me on track.

To my awesome niece and nephew, you always made me feel amazing because you always believed your Aunt had superpowers and I could fix everything.

I want to thank all my fellow Veterans that have served and who are still serving all things are possible and don't give up.

Introduction

Tammy James created this book to help veterans, family members, and advocates in successfully applying for benefits from the Department of Veterans Affairs ("VA"). This book is intended to allow users to quickly find information and to identify related resources that will help them to getting the benefits you are entitled to and deserve.

To accomplish this goal, Tammy James created VOICE4VETS, LLC a Veteran Organization to educate and assist veterans get the disability benefits they are entitled to ease the barrier of communication among the Veteran and Veteran Affairs. This book will:

Briefly describe the VA benefits process

Explain how to prepare and apply for Veteran benefits with a greater success rate

Provide suggestions to improve applications submitted to Veteran Affairs and

Table of Contents

Duty To Obtain Records

Duty to Obtain Lost or Missing Records

Duty to Provide Medical Examination

Duty to Identify Inferred Claims

Required Documents Every Veteran Should Have

Every veteran should maintain a copy of his or her DD Form 214, which is the separation paperwork issued by each branch of the service. Depending on when you served, or if you served in the Guard or Reserves, you may have a similar form which has a different form name. Whichever form you have, keep a copy of it in a safe place, as it is the key to unlocking your benefits!

Chapter 1 Eligibility for VA Benefits

Establishing Eligibility

The law currently sets three threshold conditions to be eligible for VA benefits:

1. veteran status,

2. character of discharge, and

3. a medical condition that is not the result of willful misconduct or substance abuse.

Veteran Status

Veteran status is defined as:

1. a claimant must be "a person who served in the active military services", and

2. who was discharged or released "under conditions other than dishonorable.

Character of Discharge

VA benefits are restricted to veterans discharged or released "under conditions other than dishonorable." The military services each have several categories of discharge, one of which is "dishonorable." These categories are not what VA bases a character of service determination: VA has its own unique system.

VA generally accepts **"honorable"** discharges and discharges **"under honorable conditions"** as qualifying discharges without further investigation. VA has also determined that a **"dishonorable"** discharge is not an "other than dishonorable" discharge and so will disqualify a claimant from any VA benefits unless a narrow insanity exception applies. If an individual received a discharge under "other than honorable conditions" or a "bad conduct" discharge, VA will make a special "character of service determination" before further processing a claim. In making this determination VA is supposed to consider the veteran's entire period of service not just the specific type of discharge. If VA determines that the individual was separated from service under disqualifying condition, the veteran will be ineligible for compensation benefits, although he or she may still qualify for certain healthcare benefits. A character of service determination can be appealed if unfavorable.

Veterans with multiple periods of active duty may have been discharged with a different character of service for different periods of service. In such a case, the discharge for the period of service to which a medical condition is connected controls eligibility. For example, a veteran with an honorable discharge followed by a dishonorable discharge for two separate periods of service would be eligible for benefits for a condition connected to the first period of service, but not the second.

Regardless of the character of discharge, individuals are not eligible for VA benefits for conditions that result from **"willful misconduct" or "substance abuse"**. Willful misconduct includes intentional acts such as self-inflicted injuries to avoid duty or deployment. Health conditions arising from the abuse of illegal drugs or alcohol abuse are also excluded. As questions of willful misconduct are very fact specific, claimants potentially affected by this requirement are encouraged to discuss the matter with an experienced advocate. There is one very important exception to the substance abuse exclusion. An individual is eligible for VA benefits for conditions related to drug or alcohol abuse arising from another allowable service-connected condition. For example, an individual suffering from post-traumatic stress disorder ("PTSD") because of an incident during service can receive benefits for the adverse health effects of alcoholism if the alcoholism is determined to be a result of the PTSD. **Alcoholism unrelated to another service-connected condition would not be eligible for compensation**.

VA "compensation . . . is not payable unless the period of service on which the claim is based was terminated by discharge or release under conditions other than dishonorable." 38 C.F.R. § 3.12(a). "A discharge or release because of one of the offenses specified in this paragraph is considered to have been issued under dishonorable conditions. An offense involving moral turpitude. This includes, generally, conviction of a felony." 38 C.F.R. § 3.12(d)(3). 38 U.S.C. section 101(2) defines a veteran as a person who "was discharged ... under conditions other than dishonorable."

While no statute or regulation generally states that dishonorable conditions are equivalent to conditions other than honorable, section 3.12(d)(4) states as follows:

A discharge or release because of one of the offenses specified in this paragraph is considered to have been issued under dishonorable conditions.

Willful and persistent misconduct. This includes a discharge under other than honorable conditions, if it is determined that it was issued because of willful and persistent misconduct. A discharge because of a minor offense will not, however, be considered willful and persistent misconduct if service was otherwise honest, faithful and meritorious.

Chapter 2 Compensation Benefits Overview

The following disability compensation benefits are available to Veterans:

Disability Compensation – Disability Compensation a monthly monetary benefit paid to Veterans who are disabled by an injury or disease that was incurred in or aggravated by active military service. VA and DOD offer pre-discharge programs that can help Veterans apply for disability compensation before discharge from military service. Disability compensation is a monthly tax-free benefit paid to Veterans who are at least 10% disabled because of injuries or diseases that were incurred in or aggravated during active duty or active duty for training. A disability can apply to physical conditions, such as a chronic knee condition, as well as a mental health conditions, such as post-traumatic stress disorder (PTSD).

If you were on inactive duty for training, the disability must have resulted from injury, heart attack, or stroke. Your discharge from service must have been under other than dishonorable conditions. Compensation varies depending on the degree of your disability.

PRESUMPTIVE DISABILITY BENEFITS

VA presumes that some disabilities are due to military service. You may be eligible to receive service-connected disability benefits if you have a qualifying disability associated with certain conditions of service, such as:

Veterans in the following groups may qualify for "presumptive" disability benefits:

Former prisoners of war: have a condition that is at least 10 percent disabling

Vietnam Veterans: Exposed to Agent Orange o Served in the Republic of Vietnam or on a vessel operating not more than 12 nautical miles seaward from the demarcation line of the waters of Vietnam and Cambodia between Jan. 9, 1962, and May 7, 1975.

 Atomic Veterans: Exposed to ionizing radiation and who experienced one of the following: o Participated in atmospheric nuclear testing o Occupied or were prisoners of war in Hiroshima or Nagasaki o Served before Feb. 1, 1992, at a diffusion plant in Paducah, Kentucky, Portsmouth, Ohio or Oak Ridge, Tennessee o Served before Jan. 1, 1974, at Amchitka Island, Alaska.

Gulf War Veterans: Served in the Southwest Asia Theater of Operations

Have a condition that is at least 10 percent disabling by Dec. 31, 2021, Gulf War Deployed Veterans

Served in the Southwest Theater of Operations during the Persian Gulf War
Served in Afghanistan, Syria, Djibouti, or Uzbekistan on or after September 19, 2001

Automobile Allowance – Financial assistance provided to help eligible severely disabled Service members and Veterans purchase or adapt an automobile to accommodate their disabilities. If you are a Service member or Veteran with a disability, VA may provide you with a one-time allowance to purchase a new or used car to accommodate your service-connected disability. The funds are paid directly to the seller of the automobile.

To be eligible to receive an automobile allowance, Service members or Veterans must have one of the following disabilities due to their military service:

Loss of, or permanent loss of use of one or both feet, or both hands, and

Permanent impairment of vision in both eyes that makes driving impossible even with normal corrective lenses, OR certain severe burns

You may also be eligible for assistance in purchasing adaptive equipment, such as power steering, power brakes, power windows, power seats, or other special equipment that is necessary to safely operate your vehicle if you have any of the conditions above or ankylosis (immobility of the joint) of one or both knees and hips.

Clothing Allowance – annual stipend(s) provided to disabled Veterans who have unique clothing needs because of a service-connected disability or injury. Annual stipend(s) provided to disabled Veterans who have unique clothing needs because of a service-connected disability or injury. VA can provide you with one or more annual clothing allowance payments if you are a Veteran who:

Uses a prosthetic or orthopedic device (including a wheelchair) because of a service-connected disability, AND/OR

Has a service-connected skin condition and uses a medication that causes irreparable damage to outer garments

To receive payment(s), you must establish eligibility by August 1 of the year for which you claim payment(s). To apply, contact the representative in the prosthetic department at your nearest VA medical center.

Additional VA benefits:

Specially Adapted Housing/ Special Home Adaptation Grants – provides monetary benefits to adapt or obtain suitable housing for eligible severely disabled Veterans. Specially Adapted Housing/ Special Home Adaptation Grants – provides monetary benefits to adapt or obtain suitable housing for eligible severely disabled Veterans. SHA grants help Service members and Veterans with certain service-connected disabilities adapt or purchase a home to accommodate the disability.

You can use SHA grants in one of the following ways:

Adapt an existing home the Service member, Veteran, or family member already owns in which the Service member or Veteran lives

Adapt a home the Service member, Veteran, or family member intends to purchase in which the Service member or Veteran will live

Help a Service member or Veteran purchase a home already adapted in which the Service member or Veteran will live.

Temporary Residence Assistance (TRA) Grant. TRA grants are available for Service members and Veterans who qualify for either an SAH or SHA grant to adapt the home of a family member with whom the Service member or Veteran is temporarily

Service-Disabled Veterans' Insurance (S-DVI) – provides life insurance coverage to Veterans who have been given a VA rating for a new service-connected disability in the last two years. Totally disabled Veterans are eligible for free insurance premiums and have the opportunity to purchase additional insurance

Veterans' Mortgage Life Insurance (VMLI) – provides mortgage life insurance protection to disabled Veterans who have been approved for a VA Specially Adapted Housing (SAH) Grant.

Vocational Rehabilitation and Employment (VR&E) – provides educational and training services to Veterans with service-connected illnesses and injuries to prepare for, obtain, and maintain suitable employment

Education Assistance – provides education benefits to Veterans to assist with obtaining a degree or with pursuing other eligible education and training

Dependents' Educational Assistance (DEA) – provides assistance to survivors or dependents of Veterans to obtain a degree and pursue other eligible education and training

Special Monthly Compensation. Special Monthly Compensation may be payable in addition to the basic rate of compensation when the severity of certain disabilities or combination of disabilities involves:

Loss or loss of use of specific organs, sensory functions, or extremities, OR Disabilities that confine you to your residence, OR

Disabilities that render you permanently bedridden or in need of aid and attendance, OR

Combinations of severe disabilities that significantly affect walking, OR

Existence of multiple, independent disabilities each rated at 50% or 100%, OR

Existence of multiple disabilities which, in total, render you in need of such a degree of special skilled assistance that, without it you would be permanently confined to a skilled-care nursing home

Vocational Rehabilitation and Employment (VR&E) – provides educational and training services to Veterans with service-connected illnesses and injuries to prepare for, obtain, and maintain suitable employment. VR&E is specifically for Service members and Veterans with service-connected illnesses and injuries. VA will evaluate your interests, aptitudes, abilities, and assess how your disability affects your ability to work. Effective

VR&E also provides a range of career services, including:

Career counseling and rehabilitation planning for employment as job training, job-seeking skills, résumé development, and other work-readiness assistance. »On-the-Job Training (OJT), apprenticeships, and non-paid work experiences in addition, independent living services are also available if you are so severely disabled that you are not currently ready or able to work.

Education Assistance – provides education benefits to Veterans to assist with obtaining a degree or with pursuing other eligible education and training

Dependents' Educational Assistance (DEA) – provides assistance to survivors or dependents of Veterans to obtain a degree and pursue other eligible education and training.

Chapter 3 Service-Connected Disability Compensation

Service-Connected Medical Conditions

VA is authorized to compensate eligible individuals only for "service connected" conditions. A service-connected condition is a condition caused by, aggravated by, or the result of, an event during military service or a condition considered service-connected by law (such as Section 1151 claims). As such, "service connection" is a critical concept in VA benefits law. In practice, the determination of service connection can be difficult for VA and frustrating for the veteran. As a result, service connection is one of the most contested issues in the VA claims process.

Establishing service connection generally requires:
1. Medical evidence of a current disability or condition.
2. Evidence of an in-service occurrence or aggravation of a disease or injury; and

3. Medical evidence of either a nexus between the claimed in-service disease or injury and the current disease or injury.

As a practical matter, establishing the existence of a current medical condition or disability is usually straightforward because the condition is often the motivation for filing a claim. A past condition that has been corrected or resolved or the anticipation of a future condition are not current conditions and do not provide a basis for service connection.

Next, the condition must have occurred in or resulted from the veteran's military service. In most cases, the evidence of the event (wounded by enemy action, training injury) can be found in service records, service medical records, or unit records. Under certain circumstances, a claimant may establish an in-service event by other evidence, such as "buddy statements" or testimony by other service members witnessing the event or private medical records. Whatever the case, VA will also review service medical records to determine if the claimed condition existed when the veteran entered service. If a condition is determined to be "pre-existing" and not aggravated in service, the claim will be denied.

There are also certain "presumptions" regarding specific conditions and in-service events (atomic test participation, (Agent Orange exposure) that may apply. A presumption is when the law assumes an event occurs except when there is evidence that the event did not happen. So, for veterans who were exposed to radiation during atomic bomb tests, that radiation is assumed to cause certain diseases. If the veteran now suffers from one of those diseases, he or she does not have to prove the radiation actually caused the disease: VA must accept that the disease as service connected.

Finally, VA must find a "nexus" (a "connection") between the current condition and the in-service disease, injury, or event. In practice, most service-connection issues boil down to whether a claimant can establish a nexus. For many medical conditions, such as cancer, it is extremely difficult to connect the current disease to specific events, even when occurrence of the event is not disputed. In such cases, it is especially important for the claimant to obtain strong medical evidence supporting nexus. This is not easy. Providing adequate nexus evidence becomes even more difficult as the time between service and the claim grows.

Although a condition must result from actions "in the line of duty," service-connected conditions are not limited to "battlefield" wounds or similar injuries. The "in the line of duty" requirement has been broadly interpreted to mean almost anything that occurs during service, including such things as car accidents, sports injuries, and illnesses unrelated to specific military activity. The condition generally need only have occurred or begun during service, including authorized leave periods.

Secondary Service Connection

"Secondary" service connection is awarded when a disability "is proximately due to or the result of a service-connected disease or injury." 38 C.F.R. § 3.310(a); Roper v. Nicholson, 20 Vet. App. 173, 181 (2006); Libertine v. Brown, 9 Vet. App. 521, 522 (1996); Allen v. Brown, 7 Vet. App. 439, 448 (1995) (en banc). "Proximate cause" is defined as "[t]hat which, in a natural and continuous sequence, unbroken by any efficient intervening cause, produces injury, and without which the result would not have occurred." BLACK'S LAW DICTIONARY 1225 (6th ed. 1990); Forshey v. West, 12 Vet. App. 71, 74 (1998), aff'd sub nom. Forshey v. Principi, 284 F.3d 1335 (Fed. Cir. 2002), rev'd on other grounds by Morgan v. Principi, 327 F.3d 1357 (Fed. Cir. 2003); VA Gen. Coun. Prec. 6-2003, at *3-4, n.4 (Oct. 28, 2003).).

Medical Conditions Aggravated by "Service"

VA will compensate claimants for medical conditions that existed at the time of entry into service that were made worse or "aggravated" by service. The essence of a claim for benefits based on a theory of aggravation is that a claimant's service caused a worsening of a preexisting condition.[1] See Wagner v. Principi, 370 F.3d 1089, 1096 (Fed. Cir. 2004) ("[I]f a preexisting disorder is noted upon entry into service, the veteran cannot bring a claim for service connection for that disorder, but the veteran may bring a claim for service connected aggravation of that disorder.").

An appellant may obtain service connection for aggravation of a preexisting condition under 38 U.S.C. section 1153. In such a case, "the burden falls on the veteran to establish aggravation." Wagner, 370 F.3d at 1096. If the veteran succeeds in showing aggravation, "the burden shifts to the government to show . . . that the increase in disability is due to the natural progress of the disease." Id. Where there has been an increase in disability during service, the proof that the increase was due to the natural progress of the disease must also be by clear and unmistakable evidence. 38 C.F.R. § 3.306(b). Therefore, the first task for the Board in evaluating a presumption of aggravation claim is to find whether the appellant has shown an increase in disability during service. If the Board finds aggravation, the second task is for the Board to consider whether the increased disability is due to the natural progression of the disease. See Wagner, 370 F.3d at 1096.

Schedular Ratings for Compensation

As discussed earlier, the VA compensation system is based on a "schedule" which assigns a numerical value to medical conditions from 0% to 100% in 10% increments. These "schedular ratings" are intended to represent the average percentage of impact on a veteran's employability from service-connected conditions. The smaller the impact from the condition or conditions, the lower the rating and the smaller monthly benefit paid to the veteran. A 100% rating, in theory, is granted when the service-connected condition or conditions prevent a veteran from holding any gainful employment.

A 100% rating, however, does not mean that a claimant cannot work or must quit his or her job. It only means that Congress has established that the rated condition would affect the average individual's ability to hold gainful employment. The same is true for other rating levels. The average person is considered, the specific claimant may be affected. In any event, the claimant is not penalized for working with a schedular rating. This is not true for a total disability rating based on individual unemployability discussed in the next section.

Once a veteran has been awarded service connection for a disease or disorder, VA will assign the veteran an appropriate disability rating after referring to the schedule of ratings for reductions in earning capacity for the specific injury or disability. See 38 U.S.C. § 1155. The rating is based, as far as practicable, upon the average impairments of earning capacity, in civil occupations, resulting from such injuries. Id. The Secretary has promulgated regulations to implement assignment of an appropriate disability rating. See generally 38 C.F.R. Part. 4.

VA compensation system is based on a "schedule" which assigns a numerical value to medical conditions from 0% to 100% in 10% increments. These "schedular ratings" are intended to represent the average percentage of impact on a veteran's employability from service-connected conditions. The smaller the impact from the condition or conditions, the lower the rating and the smaller monthly benefit paid to the veteran. A 100% rating, in theory, is granted when the service-connected condition or conditions prevent a veteran from holding any gainful employment.

A 100% rating, however, does not mean that a claimant cannot work or must quit his or her job. It only means that Congress has established that the rated condition would affect the average individual's ability to hold gainful employment. The same is true for other rating levels. The average person is considered, the specific claimant may be affected more or less. In any event, the claimant is not penalized for working with a schedular rating. This is not true for a total disability rating based on individual unemployability discussed in the next section.

Once a veteran has been awarded service connection for a disease or disorder, VA will assign the veteran an appropriate disability rating after referring to the schedule of ratings for reductions in earning capacity for the specific injury or disability. See 38 U.S.C. § 1155. The rating is based, as far as practicable, upon the average impairments of earning capacity, in civil occupations, resulting from such injuries. Id. The Secretary has promulgated regulations to implement assignment of an appropriate disability rating. See generally 38 C.F.R. Part. 4.

After consideration of these factors and based on all the evidence of record that bears on occupational and social impairment, VA must assign a disability rating that most closely reflects the level of social and occupational impairment a veteran is suffering. See, e.g., 38 C.F.R. § 4.126. Where there is a question as to which of two evaluations to apply, the Board will assign the higher rating if a veteran's disability more closely resembles the criteria for the higher rating; otherwise, the lower rating will be assigned. See 38 C.F.R. § 4.7; see also, e.g., Mauerhan v. Principi, 16 Vet. App. 436, 440-41 (2002) (discussing PTSD rating issues).

The amount of VA compensation due to a claimant is determined by evaluation of the disability or disabilities resulting from diseases and injuries encountered because of or incident to military service. 38 C.F.R. § 4.1. "VA's rating schedule is constructed for the purpose of establishing levels of disability for compensation purposes based upon 'average impairment in earning capacity' resulting from particular injuries or diseases." Mitchell v. Shinseki, 25 Vet. App. 32, 36 (2011); Hensley v. Brown, 5 Vet. App. 155, 162 (1993) (quoting 38 U.S.C. § 1155); 38 C.F.R. § 4.1. VA regulations also caution that "it is not expected . . . that all cases will show all the findings specified in the [applicable disability code]." 38 C.F.R. § 4.21.

Schedular Rating 100%-Total and Permanent

Schedular Rating 100%-Total and Permanent

If any one of the Veteran's disabilities qualifies for a 100 percent rating under the rating schedule, the total disability requirement for pension is satisfied. Under VA disability compensation only service-connected disabilities are considered for the total and permanent rating.

Schedular Rating 100%-TDIU or Individual Unemployability

In some cases, however, a veteran with less than a 100% scheduler rating is so affected by service-connected conditions that he or she cannot work at gainful employment. The law allows for another type of claim in such a case.

VA benefits are available to compensate a veteran at the 100% level if he or she is not able to work because of service-connected conditions even without a 100% schedular rating. This benefit is called "total disability based on individual unemployability", ("TDIU"), or sometimes "individual unemployability," ("IU").

The key issue in a TDIU claim is the inability of the veteran to engage in "substantially gainful employment" because of his or her service-connected conditions. "Substantially gainful employment" means to hold a job that pays at least an amount equal to the annual poverty level set by the federal government. To qualify for TDIU benefits, a claimant must meet the following requirements:

1. If the claimant has only one service-connected condition, that condition must be schedular rated at least 60% or more.
2. If the claimant has two or more service-connected conditions, at least one of those conditions must be rated at 40% or more, and the veteran's combined disability rating must be 70% or more; and
3. In either case, the veteran must be unemployable because of his or her service-connected conditions.

To establish "unemployability" or "inability to substantially maintain gainful employment", the Veteran must provide:

1. Evidence of unemployment due to service-connected conditions, employment history records for example, and
2. Medical evidence that the veteran's service-connected condition renders him or her totally disabled and unemployable, generally a doctor's opinion letter.

Having a paying job does not automatically disqualify a claimant from a TDIU award. If the wages are considered "marginal" (low paying) or "sheltered" (protected from usual requirements) employment are exceptions to the TDIU qualification requirements. Examples of employment that are allowed under TIDU:

1. A job that pays substantially less than the prevailing poverty level,
2. A job that is protected from requirements that someone else in that position would be expected to satisfy, or
3. A job working for a friend or relative, may not be "substantially gainful employment."

Although it is always better to submit a specific claim for TDIU. The VA has a duty to look for potential TDIU claims based on the evidence in the claimant's VA claims file, known as a "C-file". The VA is required to review the claims for TIDU, even if not specifically requested by the Veteran, because entitlement to TDIU is part of every claim for disability compensation. Upon reviewing the claim, the VA determines if TDIU is an appropriate award for the claim. Evidence of unemployability can be submitted after an initial decision denying TDIU, if while a claim for schedular benefits is still being processed.

As with most VA benefits, TDIU is not a permanent benefit. The VA can require a claimant undergo periodic medical examinations to confirm that the claimant remains unable to work due to a service-connected condition. And, as with all VA examinations, a failure to report for a scheduled examination can result in suspension or termination of a TDIU benefits.

In addition, since a TDIU award is also based on "unemployability," the VA can periodically request employment information from a claimant receiving TDIU benefits. The VA will also cross check employment earnings with the IRS.

The TDIU rating could be terminated, and the claimant could be liable to repay VA for the TDIU benefits paid since that employment began, if:

1. the VA becomes aware that a claimant is working at a job that is not marginal or sheltered,
2. A claimant must also be careful in performing volunteer work because the nature and time spent at unpaid work shows that a claimant could be employed and is no longer unemployable.

If a Veteran is determined to be employable, the **TDIU award can and will probably be revoked**. When a TDIU rating is revoked, a claimant's benefits go back to the amount of compensation payable under the scheduler rating and the VA can make the Veteran repay the TDIU award.

Schedular Rating 100%-Temporary Disability Rating

Temporary 100% Disability Rating

There are three types of temporary disability ratings:
•**Prestabilization Ratings**
•**Total Ratings for Service-Connected Disability Requiring Hospitalization**
•**Convalescence Rating (TDCC)**

Prestabilization Ratings:
•Prestabilization Rating of 100% is for Veterans who have experienced, during active, an unstable condition resulting in a severe disability that renders gainful employment either not feasible or advisable. Such conditions would include residuals resulting from a head injury or gunshot wound residuals.
•The VA is not allowed to assign a 100% prestabilization rating if the Veteran's case warrants a 100% regular rating.

•Assigned immediately after discharge from the military and continues for 12 months after discharge.

•During the 12 months, the Prestabilized rating can change to a "another rating authorizing a greater benefit" if the change would be a better benefit for the Veteran.

•There must be a VA exam of the Veteran between the 6 month and the 12-month following discharge. If the exam calls for a reduction in benefits, the VA cannot make the reduction until the end of 12-month period.

Total Ratings for Service-Connected Disabilities Requiring Hospitalization

•The condition must be service connected.

•The period of hospitalization or observation must exceed 21 days.

•The Increased rating starts on the first day of continuous hospitalization and ends on the last day of the month of hospital discharge.

•If hospitalization occurs for a non-service-connected condition and during the hospitalization a service connected disability is treated for over 21 days, then the 100% can be granted.

Convalescence Rating (TDCC):

•Three circumstances for TDCC: ◦The Veteran has surgery that requires 1 month of convalescence, or

◦The Veteran's surgery has resulted in severe postoperative residuals, or

◦The Veteran has a major joint immobilized by a cast.

•Convalescence for Mental Disorder: ◦Veteran must have a service-connected mental disorder

◦Hospitalized for at least 6months for the service-connected mental disorder

◦Convalescent rating will last for 6 months after hospital discharge. This rating is protected under 38 C.F.R. 3.105(e)

•Benefit is for up to a year.

•The conditions must be service connected, and the medical documentation indicates that the Veteran needs time to convalesce after hospital discharge or outpatient release.

•Home Confinement is not necessary. Ruling from Felden v. West, defines convalescence as "the act of regaining or returning to a normal or healthy state after a surgical operation, or injury" Medical documentation is necessary. If Veteran's doctor prescribes: "Do not return to work for 12 weeks", then the CAVC has ruled that the note establishes 12 weeks of convalescence.

Compensation Rates

Compensation rates are established by Congress. The VA compensation system is based on the rated percentage of disability ("scheduler rating") and not on the rank of the veteran at time of discharge. At present, a senior officer and a junior enlisted who are each rated as 30% disabled each will receive the same amount of compensation per month from VA. At one time the amount of VA benefits payable for the same condition was different depending on whether the veteran served in a time of war or not. Under the current payment schedule, compensation benefits for both classes of veterans are the same. So, veterans with the same percent rated disability today receive the same monetary compensation regardless of when they served. [link to 38 USC 1110 v. 1131]. 38 U.S.C. section 1114 sets forth the compensation rates for all awards of disability compensation, whether based on a new claim or a claim retroactively granted based on CUE in a prior VA decision. When the rates are set by Congress, they have a specific effective date and remain in effect until they are changed. Nothing in the statute provides for payment of a higher rate when the payments are retroactive, and the Court cannot find any intent for payment at the higher rate without a clear, explicit waiver of the Government's sovereign immunity from the payment of interest. 38 U.S.C § 1114; *see also Smith v. Principi,* 281 F.3d 1384, 1387 (Fed. Cir. 2002) ("waiver of the no-interest rule must be express"). Further, the suggestion that section 1114 requires that an award of retroactive benefits must be calculated at the rate in effect at the time of payment was expressly rejected by the Federal Circuit in *Sandstrom v. Principi*, 358 F.3d 1376, 1380 (Fed. Cir. 2004).

Thus, a claimant is not entitled to receive an amount not authorized by Congress during a particular time frame.

Special Monthly Compensation (SMC)

In addition to compensation based on the degree of disability, Congress has also authorized additional compensation for certain disabilities. This "special monthly compensation" ("SMC") is intended to compensate claimants for service-connected conditions that involve loss of use or anatomical loss (amputation) of body parts, such as hands or feet, or loss of hearing or sight. SMC can result in significantly more monthly compensation for severely injured veterans.

While a scheduler rating depends on the severity of a condition, SMC for loss of use does not depend on the degree of loss, except that the loss of use must be permanent. The more seriously disabled veteran may be eligible for SMC payments for combinations of anatomical loss or loss of use. In addition, severely disabled veterans may be awarded further compensation for regular aid and attendance needs and for permanent housebound conditions. As SMC has many possible combinations and involves a significant amount of additional compensation

Levels of SMC Ratings

Each level of SMC ratings is successive and are preceded by an entitlement to certain conditions included under SMC (K). The basic elements of Special Monthly Compensation ratings include:

•anatomical (or physical) loss or the loss of use (Loss of use from neurological, muscular, vascular, contractures, etc.) Of one or more of the following:

Limbs,

Hands, feet,

Reproductive organs,

Aphonia (loss of voice)

Deafness

Blindness

Loss of bowel and bladder control

Being permanently housebound

and a need for regular aid and attendance with activities of daily living or a higher level of care. All of which must be a result of the veteran's service-connected disabilities.

A rating of SMC (K) would include:

The anatomical loss or loss of use (Loss of use from neurological, muscular, vascular, contractures, etc.) of:

one hand.

one foot.

both buttocks (where the applicable bilateral muscle group prevents the individual from maintaining unaided upright posture, rising, and stooping actions).

◦one or more creative organs used for reproduction (absence of testicles, ovaries, or other creative organ, ¼ loss of tissue of a single breast or both breasts in combination) due to trauma while in service, or as a residual of a service-connected disability(ies). NOTE: these do not serve as eligible prerequisite conditions for the higher levels of SMC.

One eye (loss of use to include specific levels of blindness).

Complete organic aphonia (constant loss of voice due to disease)

Deafness of both ears to include absence of air and bone conduction.

A rating of SMC (L) would include:

The anatomical loss or loss of use of:

Both feet,

One hand and one foot

Blindness in both eyes with visual acuity of 5/200 and less.

Permanently bedridden.

Regular need for aid and attendance to assist with activities of daily living such as dressing oneself, tending to personal hygiene, care and adjustment of assistive appliances or prosthetics, feeding oneself, and the like. (Specific criteria is established in 38 CFR § 3.352(a)) (NOTE: If such services are not being provided at the expense of the U.S. Government due to hospitalization).

Ratings above the SMC (L) level to include SMC (M), SMC (N), SMC(O), SMC(P), SMC(R) and SMC(S) are specialized multifaceted levels which are based on various specific combinations of anatomical loss or loss of use of designated extremities and/or senses, together with seriously disabling conditions and particular degrees of aid and attendance requirements, housebound or bedridden statuses deemed medically necessary, and explicit service-connection ratings. These levels also outline various requirements to include full and half step upgraded SMC level ratings. The conditions providing the basis of these levels are as follows.

A rating of SMC (M) would include:

•The anatomical loss or loss of use of (neurological loss):

◦Both hands,

◦Both legs at the region of the knee

◦One arm at the region of the elbow with one leg at the region of the knee

•Blindness in both eyes having only light perception.

•Blindness in both eyes resulting in the need for regular aid and attendance.

A rating of SMC (N) would include:

•The anatomical loss or loss of use of both arms at the region of the elbow.

•The anatomical loss of both legs so near the hip that it prevents the use of a prosthetic appliance.

•The anatomical loss of one arm so near the shoulder that it prevents the use of a prosthetic appliance along with the anatomical loss of one leg so near the hip that it prevents the use of a prosthetic appliance.

•The anatomical loss of both eyes and blindness in both eyes to include loss of light perception.

A rating of SMC (O) would include:

•The anatomical loss of both arms so near the shoulder that it prevents the use of a prosthetic appliance.

•Bilateral deafness rated at least 60 percent disabling along with service-connected blindness with visual acuity of 20/200 or less of both eyes.

•Complete deafness in one ear or bilateral deafness rated at least 40 percent disabling along with service-connected blindness in both eyes to include loss of light perception.

•Paraplegia – paralysis of both lower extremities along with bowel and bladder incontinence.

•Helplessness due to a combination of anatomical loss or loss of use or two extremities with deafness and blindness or a combination of multiple injuries causing severe and total disability.

A rating of SMC (P) would include:

•The anatomical loss or loss of use of a leg at or below the knee along with the anatomical loss or loss of use of the other leg at a level above the knee.

•The anatomical loss or loss of use of a leg below the knee along with the anatomical loss or loss of use of an arm above the elbow.

•The anatomical loss or loss of use of one leg above the knee and the anatomical loss or loss of use of a hand.

•Blindness in both eyes meeting the requirements outlined in SMC (L), (M) or (N) levels.

A rating of SMC(R):

Ratings under SMC(R) are assigned for seriously disabled veterans in need of advanced levels of aid and attendance.

SMC(R) ratings require a minimal combination of entitlement to both SMC(O) and SMC(L). Additionally, Veterans in receipt of SMC rates based on Aid and Attendance are strongly advised to contact their service representative and/or VA Regional Office should they become hospitalized at the expense of the U.S. Government (i.e. a VA medical facility) as failure to do so could create an overpayment of monetary benefits.

A rating of SMC(S):

Ratings under SMC(S) are also available if the veteran is permanently housebound. The VA defines "permanently housebound" as being substantially (as opposed to completely) confined to a dwelling as the result of service-connected disability and it is reasonably certain that that such disability will continue throughout the veteran's lifetime. These kinds of determinations should be made by a physician, whose written opinions or reports in this respect would serve as the best evidence to submit in support of a claim for "s" SMC benefits.

A rating of SMC(T): Traumatic Brain Injury

Ratings under SMC(T) are available to veterans who need regular aid A&A for residuals of Traumatic Brain Injury (TBI) but is not eligible for a higher level of A&A under (R)(2), and would require hospitalization, nursing home care, or other residential institutional care in absence of regular in-home aid and attendance.

CHAPTER 4 Types of VA Claims

1. Elements of a Claim

A claim is "a formal or informal communication in writing requesting a determination of entitlement or evidencing a belief in entitlement, to a benefit." Hillyard v. Shinseki, 24 Vet. App. 343, 355 (2011) (citing 38 C.F.R. § 3.1). For initial claims, a "specific claim in the form prescribed by the Secretary must be filed in order for benefits to be paid to any individual under the laws administered by VA." 38 C.F.R. § 3.150(a); 38 U.S.C. § 5101(a). Subsequent applications for additional claims or increases do not require use of the form. The law is clear for initial claims, however, that only the approved VA form (currently VA Form 21-526) is acceptable as a formal application for compensation or pension benefits. Whatever the means, the essential elements for any claim, whether formal or informal, are:

(1) an intent to apply for benefits

(2) an identification of the benefits sought; and

(3) a communication in writing.

A "claimant has the responsibility to present and support a claim for benefits under laws administered by the Secretary." 38 U.S.C. § 5107(a). Further, VA has no duty to provide notice to claimants to file claims for service connection, and a claimant is bound by governing regulations.

Formal VA Claim

A formal VA claim is any claim that is filed using a VA form. The VA states that the "original claim" is the first formal claim for a claimant on a prescribed VA application form. There is only one original claim per claimant. The two "original claim" forms are:

VA Form 21-526 Veteran's Application for Compensation or Pension, or

VA Form 21-526EZ Application for Disability Compensation and Related Compensation Benefits which must be submitted with a Fully Developed Claim.

After the "original claim" has been filed and a decision has been made by a VA Rating Officer, RO, all future pension, or compensation claims, even if not related to the original claim, are referred to as "reopened claims". Future claims can be processed by using either VA form 21-526(b) Supplemental Claim Compensation: increase, new, secondary, service-connected conditions or reopens or VA 21-4138 Statement of Support.

2. Informal VA Claims

Any written communication from a claimant that indicates an intent to apply for an identified benefit may be considered an informal claim. See Norris v. West, 12 Vet. App. 413, 421 (1999); 38 C.F.R. § 3.155(a). Even an informal claim for benefits must be in writing. There are three requirements that must be satisfied if the Board is to find that an informal claim has been filed. There must be (1) a communication in writing that (2) expresses an intent to apply for benefits, and (3) identifies the benefits sought.

A VA medical report can qualify as an informal claim when ... a claimant's formal claim for compensation has already been allowed, receipt of ... a VA report of examination will be accepted as an informal claim filed on the date of the examination." 38 C.F.R. § 3.157(b); Servello v. Derwinski, 3 Vet. App. 196, 198, 200 (1992); Norris v. West, 12 Vet. App. 413 (1999).

In addition, certain medical records demonstrating a worsening in a veteran's disability that is already service connected may constitute an informal claim for an increased disability rating for that disability. 38 C.F.R. § 3.157(b); see Massie v. Shinseki, 25 Vet. App. 123, 131-32 (2011) (discussing the requirements of § 3.157(b)). A medical report will be considered an informal claim only "when such report [] relate[s] to examination or treatment of a disability for which service-connection has previously been established." MacPhee, 459 F.3d at 1328 (quoting 38 C.F.R. § 3.157(b) (1)). The determination of whether an informal claim has been filed is a substantially factual determination that the Court reviews under the "clearly erroneous" standard of review. Brokowski, 23 Vet. App. at 85; see 38 U.S.C. § 7261(a) (4); Ellington v. Nicholson, 22 Vet. App. 141, 144 (2007), aff'd, 541 F.3d 1364 (Fed. Cir. 2008). Because medical records documenting symptoms alone cannot, as a matter of law, raise initial claims for VA benefits for conditions characterized by symptoms, VA is not obligated to consider this possibility. Criswell, 20 Vet. App. at 503-04; see also 38 U.S.C. § 7104(d)(1) (requiring VA to consider only the "material issues of . . . law presented on the record").

3. Inferred VA Claims

An "inferred" claim is one not specifically identified by a claimant but supported by the evidence. Once a claim is received, VA has a duty to review the claim and the C-file supporting documents, and oral testimony in a liberal manner to identify and adjudicate all reasonably raised claims, even if a specific claim is not raised by the appellant. See Shockley v. West, 11 Vet. App. 208, 214 (1998); see also Collier v. Derwinski, 2 Vet. App. 247, 251 (1992) (holding that although the appellant had not filed the specific form asking for individual unemployability, an informal claim was raised because he had continually stated he was unable to work due to his service-connected mental disorder). This is discussed elsewhere in this Knowledge Book. Claimants should not rely on this duty and should always identify all the claims he or she believes are supported by the evidence.

Chapter 5 Filing Claim-Evidentiary Issues

1. Evidentiary Issues

The Board may draw a reasonable inference from a lack of notation of a condition in a medical report, if the report would be expected to carry such information. Buczynski v. Shinseki, 24 Vet. App. 221, 224 (2011).

2. New & Material Evidence

When a claim is pending and new material evidence is received prior to the expiration of the appeals period, such evidence will be considered as having been filed in connection with the pending claim. New and material evidence "can be neither cumulative nor redundant of the evidence of record at the time of the last prior final denial." 38 C.F.R. § 3.156(a). "VA must assess any evidence submitted during the relevant period and make a determination as to whether it constitutes new and material evidence relating to the old claim." Bond v. Shinseki, 659 F.3d 1362, 1367 (2011) (emphasis added). This determination must be explicit. Id. at 1368. "This obligation persists even where . . . the RO has concluded that the submission in question also supports a new claim for an increased rating, for neither law—nor logic—dictates that evidence supporting a new claim cannot also constitute new and material evidence relating to a pending claim." Bond, 659 F.3d 1367-68. The Board's determination of whether a claimant has submitted new and material evidence is generally reviewed under the "clearly erroneous" standard of review set forth in 38 U.S.C. § 7261(a)(4). Suaviso v. Nicholson, 19 Vet. App. 532, 533-34 (2006); Elkins v. West, 12 Vet. App. 209, 217 (1999) (en banc).

3. Lay Evidence

When adjudicating a claim for veteran's benefits, "[t]he Secretary shall consider all information and lay and medical evidence of record." 38 U.S.C. § 5107(b). Lay evidence may be competent to prove the existence of a chronic disease that can be diagnosed or demonstrated without medical expertise in presumptive service-connection claims. See Savage v. Gober, 10 Vet. App. 488, 495 (1997) (for certain chronic diseases, lay evidence may be competent to identify in-service existence of chronic disease and whether current condition is subsequent manifestation of that same chronic disease); 38 C.F.R. §§ 3.303(b), 3.307(a), 3.309(a). The distinction between the use of lay evidence in direct service-connection claims and presumptive service-connection claims for chronic diseases exists because in the latter case the lay evidence is not being used to establish a medical causation or etiology but rather to establish, by evidence of observable symptomatology, that the currently diagnosed chronic disease is the same condition that was present during service or during the presumptive period of § 3.307(a).

Further, lay evidence may be competent to show continuity of symptomatology under 38 C.F.R. § 3.303(b). See Davidson v. Shinseki, 581 F.3d 1313, 1315-16 (Fed. Cir. 2009) (rejecting the view that "competent medical evidence is required ... [when] the determinative issue involves either medical etiology or a medical diagnosis." (Citing Jandreau, 492 F.3d at 1376-77)); Savage v. Gober, 10 Vet. App. 488, 497 (1997). When considering lay evidence, the Board should determine whether the veteran's disability is the type of disability for which lay evidence is competent. See Jandreau, 492 F.3d at 1377. If the disability is of the type for which lay evidence is competent, the Board must weigh that evidence against the other evidence of record in making its determination regarding the existence of a service connection. Buchanan, 451 F.3d at 1334-37.

4. Expert Opinions

"When, in the judgment of the Secretary, expert medical opinion, in addition to that available within the Department, is warranted by the medical complexity or controversy involved ... the Secretary may secure an advisory medical opinion from one or more independent medical experts who are not employees of the Department." 38 U.S.C. § 5109(a) (emphasis added); see also 38 U.S.C. § 7109(a).

The determination that an expert medical opinion is warranted is left entirely to the discretion of the Secretary. 38 U.S.C. § 7261(a)(3)(A); see Boutwell v. West, 11 Vet. App. 387, 391 (1998); Stringham v. Brown, 8 Vet. App. 445, 448 (1995).

CHAPTER 6   VA Compensation-Service Connected Disability Conditions due to Legal Presumptions

What's a Legal Presumption?

A presumption is a rule of law which permits a court to assume a fact is true without any evidence until there is a certain weight of evidence which rebuts (disproves or outweighs) the presumption. Each presumption is based upon a particular set of apparent facts coupled with established laws, logic, or reasoning. A presumption is "rebuttable" when a person can present facts to persuade a judge that the presumption is not true in his or her case. The VA system includes several presumptions some favorable and some unfavorable to claimants, as described below.

Presumption of In-service Occurrence

Congress has specified several conditions the diagnosis of which within certain periods after discharge from service gives rise to a statutory presumption of incurrence in service. 38 U.S.C. § 1112(a)(1); Collamore v. Derwinski, 2 Vet. App. 541, 543 (1992). These presumptions include:

a chronic or tropical disease developing a 10% or more degree of disability within 1 year

active tuberculosis developing a 10% or more degree of disability within 3 years

Hansen's disease developing a 10% or more degree of disability within 3 years

multiple sclerosis developing a 10% or more degree of disability within 7 years

38 U.S.C. § 1112(a). There is also a broad presumption for prisoners of war detained for not less than 30 days. 38 U.S.C. § 1112(b).

Presumption of Soundness

Every veteran shall be taken to have been in sound condition when examined, accepted, and enrolled for service, except as to defects, infirmities, or disorders noted at the time of the examination, acceptance, and enrollment. Therefore, when no preexisting medical condition is noted upon entry into service, a veteran is presumed to have been sound. The burden then falls on VA to rebut the presumption of soundness.

Agent Orange

Agent Orange was a tactical herbicide the U.S. military used to clear leaves and vegetation for military operations mainly during the Vietnam War. Veterans who were exposed to Agent Orange may have certain related illnesses.

If you have an illness caused by exposure to Agent Orange during military service, read below to find out if you may be eligible for disability compensation and how to apply.

VA's Presumption of Exposure to Agent Orange

In response to the many Vietnam-era veterans experiencing health-related concerns due to herbicide exposure, the Agent Orange Act of 1991 was passed. The Act established a presumption of service connection, meaning that VA must assume that veterans who served during certain time periods in predetermined locations were exposed to Agent Orange.

A presumption of exposure replaces the element of service connection that requires veterans to provide proof of an in-service event, injury, or illness that led to their current disability. Instead, VA considers herbicide exposure (i.e., Agent Orange) to be the in-service event for any veteran who served in the following locations during the specified timeframes:

Boots-on-the-ground in Vietnam, veterans with service aboard a ship that operated in the inland waterways of Vietnam (i.e., Brown Water veterans), or veterans with service aboard a ship in Vietnam's territorial seas (i.e., Blue Water Navy veterans) between January 9, 1962, and May 7, 1975

On or near the Korean demilitarized zone (DMZ) between September 1, 1967, and August 31, 1971

Active duty and reservist personnel who had regular contact with C-123 aircraft between 1969 and 1986.

Presumptive Service Connection for Certain Conditions Associated with Agent Orange Exposure

In addition, the Agent Orange Act created a presumption of service connection. Presumptive service connection means that veterans do not have to prove a medical nexus between their condition and their military service.

If their service meets one of the above criteria and their condition is included in VA's list of presumptive conditions, VA will grant service connection. The Act also gave the Secretary of the Department of Veterans Affairs the power to add conditions to this list over time through the creation of new regulations.

VA presumes service connection for the following Agent Orange-related conditions:

AL Amyloidosis

Chronic B-Cell Leukemia

Chloracne (if it presents within one year of exposure to a degree of 10 percent disabling)

Diabetes Mellitus Type 2

Hodgkin's Disease

Ischemic Heart Disease (including coronary artery disease, stable and unstable angina, myocardial infarction, and sudden cardiac death)

Multiple Myeloma

Non-Hodgkin's Lymphoma

Parkinson's Disease

Peripheral Neuropathy, Early Onset (if it presents within one year of exposure to a degree of 10 percent disabling)

Porphyria Cutanea Tarda (if it presents within one year of exposure to a degree of 10 percent disabling)

Prostate Cancer

Respiratory Cancers, including Lung Cancer

Soft Tissue Sarcomas (other than osteosarcoma, chondrosarcoma, Kaposi's sarcoma, and mesothelioma)

Congress Adds New Presumptive Conditions to VA's List

As mentioned above, the passing of the **2021 NDAA** means that Congress has bypassed VA and determined, by statute, the link between three new medical conditions and Agent Orange exposure. These conditions, which are now part of the list of presumptive conditions, include:

Bladder cancer

Hypothyroidism: A condition in which thyroid gland does not produce enough of certain crucial hormones.

Parkinson's-like symptoms: A condition with symptoms such as tremor, slow movement, impaired speech, and muscle stiffness that resembles Parkinson's Disease but is not formally diagnosed as such.

Changes based on Blue Water Navy Vietnam Veterans Act of 2019

Blue Water Navy Veterans who served aboard ships in the open waters off the coast of Vietnam during the Vietnam War are now presumed to be exposed to Agent Orange. If we denied your claim in the past, you can file a new claim based on Public Law 116-23.

Children of U.S. Veterans who served in Thailand during the Vietnam War may now be eligible for benefits. If your child was diagnosed with spina bifida (except spina bifida occulta), learn more about eligibility for birth defects linked to Agent Orange.

Am I eligible for VA disability benefits based on exposure to Agent Orange?

You may be eligible for VA disability benefits if you meet both requirements listed below.

Both must be true. You:

Have an illness that is caused by exposure to Agent Orange, and

Served in a location that exposed you to Agent Orange.

Requirements for Agent Orange presumptive diseases

When sound medical and scientific evidence shows that an illness is caused by Agent Orange exposure, we add it to our list of presumptive diseases. If you have been diagnosed with one of these illnesses, you don't need to prove that it started during—or got worse because of—your military service.

Service requirements for presumption of exposure:

Eligibility for VA disability compensation benefits, in part, on whether you served in a location that exposed you to Agent Orange. VA will call this having a presumption of exposure.

You have a presumption of exposure if you meet at least one of the service requirements listed below.

Between January 9, 1962, and May 7, 1975, you must have served for any length of time in at least one of these locations:

In the Republic of Vietnam, or

Aboard a U.S. military vessel that operated in the inland waterways of Vietnam, or

On a vessel operating not more than 12 nautical miles seaward from the demarcation line of the waters of Vietnam and Cambodia, or

On regular perimeter duty on the fenced-in perimeters of a U.S. Army installation in Thailand or a Royal Thai Air Force base. These bases include U-Tapao, Ubon, Nakhon Phanom, Udorn, Takhli, Korat, or Don Muang.

Or at least one of these must be true. You:

Served in or near the Korean DMZ for any length of time between September 1, 1967, and August 31, 1971, or

Served on active duty in a regular Air Force unit location where a C-123 aircraft with traces of Agent Orange was assigned, and had repeated contact with this aircraft due to your flight, ground, or medical duties, or

Were involved in transporting, testing, storing, or other uses of Agent Orange during your military service, or

Were assigned as a Reservist to certain flight, ground, or medical crew duties at one of the below locations.

Eligible Reserve locations, time periods, and units include:

Lockbourne/Rickenbacker Air Force Base in Ohio, 1969 to 1986 (906th and 907th Tactical Air Groups or 355th and 356th Tactical Airlift Squadrons)

Westover Air Force Base in Massachusetts, 1972 to 1982 (731st Tactical Air Squadron and 74th Aeromedical Evacuation Squadron, or 901st Organizational Maintenance Squadron)

Pittsburgh International Airport in Pennsylvania, 1972 to 1982 (758th Airlift Squadron)

BLUE WATER NAVY VETERANS

The presumption of herbicide exposure also applies for Navy veterans who served on vessels that were originally designated as offshore, or "blue water," vessels, but nevertheless conducted operations on the inland "brown water" rivers and delta areas of Vietnam. When a veteran alleges exposure to herbicides during service aboard a Navy or Coast Guard ship that operated on the offshore waters of Vietnam, VA is required to look for:

Evidence that shows the ship docked to the shores or piers of the RVN

operated temporarily on the RVN inland waterways, or operated on close coastal waters for extended periods, with evidence that crew members went ashore, or smaller vessels from the ship went ashore regularly with supplies or personnel evidence that places the veteran onboard the ship at the time the ship docked to the shore or pier or operated in inland waterways or on close coastal waters for extended periods, and the veteran's statement as to whether he or she went ashore when the ship docked or operated on close coastal waters for extended periods, if the evidence shows the ship docked to the shore or pier or that crew members were sent ashore when the ship operated on close coastal waters.

Combat

Claimants seeking compensation for conditions that are the result of combat have a reduced evidentiary burden (sometimes called the "**combat presumption**"). Where a veteran "engaged in combat with the enemy in active service . . . the Secretary shall accept as sufficient proof of service-connection of any disease or injury alleged to have been incurred in or aggravated by such service satisfactory lay or other evidence of service incurrence of aggravation." 38 U.S.C. 1154(b); see also 38 C.F.R. § 3.304(d)

Prisoners of War (POWs)

The law identifies certain diseases for which service connection will be rebuttably presumed for a veteran who was a prisoner of war (POW) for not less than 30 days. See 38 C.F.R. §§ 3.307, 3.309(c). Conditions subject to presumptive service connection for POWs are listed under 38 U.S.C. section 1112(b)(4). However, the presumption is rebutted "[w]here there is affirmative evidence to the contrary, or evidence to establish that an intercurrent injury or disease which is a recognized cause of [such disease], has been suffered between the date of separation from service and the onset of [the] disease." 38 U.S.C. § 1113(a); see also 38 C.F.R. § 3.307(d).

Radiation-exposed Veterans

Qualification under the presumptive provision of 38 U.S.C. section 1112(c) occurs when a veteran suffers from one of the fifteen listed cancers, and establishes participation in a "radiation risk activity" defined as:

(i)   Onsite participation in a test involving the atmospheric detonation of a nuclear device.

(ii)   The occupation of Hiroshima or Nagasaki, Japan, by United States forces during the period beginning on August 6, 1945 and ending on July 1, 1946.

(iii) Internment as prisoner of war in Japan (or service on active duty in Japan immediately following such internment) during World War II which (as determined by the Secretary) resulted in an opportunity for exposure to ionizing radiation comparable to that of veterans described in clause (ii) of this subparagraph.

Gulf War Veterans

38 C.F.R. §§ 3.317(c), (e) (1). The Southwest Asia Theater of operations refers to Iraq, Kuwait, Saudi Arabia, the neutral zone between Iraq and Saudi Arabia, Bahrain, Qatar, the United Arab Emirates, Oman, the Gulf of Aden, the Gulf of Oman, the Persian Gulf, the Arabian Sea, the Red Sea, and the airspace above these locations. 38 C.F.R. § 3.317(e)(2).

A veteran who served in Southwest Asia can be service connected for "undiagnosed illness" without direct evidence of a nexus between his or her service and the illness. For the purposes of this section, **Southwest Asia includes Iraq, Kuwait, Saudi Arabia, Bahrain, Qatar, UAE, Oman, the Gulf of Aden, the Gulf of Oman, the Persian Gulf, the Arabian Sea, the Red Sea, and the airspace above. VA also considers service in Afghanistan to be included.**

A veteran having service in any of these areas since August 2, 1990, is considered eligible for presumptive service connection for one or more of the following "manifestations:"

An undiagnosed illness is a medically unexplained chronic multisymptom condition (such as fibromyalgia, chronic fatigue syndrome, or irritable bowel syndrome; or

One of a lists of infectious diseases determined by the VA, which includes leishmaniasis

A veteran who served on active military, naval, or air service in the Southwest Asia Theater of operations during the Persian Gulf War is entitled to presumptive service connection for the following conditions:

Brucellosis

Campylobacter jejuni

Coxiella burnetii (Q fever)

Malaria

Mycobacterium tuberculosis

Nontyphoid Salmenella

Shigella

Visceral leishmaniasis

West Nile virus

Finally, for an undiagnosed illness or medically unexplained illness the condition must have manifested itself during service or to a "degree of 10 percent or more during the presumptive period, which is continuing since August 1990. For infectious diseases the presumptive period varies by disease from one year to no time limit.

For "undiagnosed" and "multisymptom" diseases that do not have their own rating tables, the issue of which condition is "similar" to the claimant's condition can mean the difference between an award and denial. VA is required to explain why they used a particular table and must consider the claimant's specific symptoms. Using the wrong rating table can unfairly prevent a 10% rating.

Veterans of the Persian Gulf with a health concern are eligible for an examination, whether or not he or she has a current condition. Persons undergoing the examination are added to the **VA Persian Gulf War Veterans Health Registry**. This registry allows VA to track Persian Gulf Veterans health conditions and, hopefully, detect conditions related to service in that theater that should be added to the presumptive list.

Certain Chronic Diseases

As discussed above, statutes and regulations governing presumptive service connection for chronic diseases, provide that such conditions which manifest within the presumptive period "shall be considered to have been incurred in or aggravated by such service, notwithstanding there is no record of evidence of such disease during the period of service." 38 U.S.C. § 1112(a) (emphasis added); see also 38 C.F.R. §§ 3.307(a)(3), 3.309(a). The law provides for presumptive service connection for various chronic diseases—designated in section 3.309(a)— if compensable manifestations of the chronic disease occur within one year of discharge from service. 38 C.F.R. § 3.307(a)(3). Evidence of the existence of a chronic disease during the applicable one-year presumption period allows for an award of service-connection.

Chapter 7 Compensation Claims-Special Rules

Special Rules for Certain Claims

Congress, and in some cases VA, has recognized that some conditions resulting from service are so widespread or unique that they require special procedures. Two of the most common of these conditions, herbicide exposure in Vietnam Era veterans and undiagnosed or multisymptom illnesses in Persian Gulf War veterans, are described below.

1. Herbicide-Exposed Veterans

Congress has established a "presumption" of exposure to herbicides, most infamously including "Agent Orange," for veterans who served in the Republic of Vietnam during the period from January 9, 1962, to May 7, 1975. A presumption is a legal term that means that VA has to assume a fact unless there is evidence against the fact. For Vietnam veterans this means that evidence of actual exposure Agent Orange is not required – those veterans is presumed to have been exposed to Agent Orange – if they meet the requirements for the presumption.

For claimants, this means that if a veteran can show he or she was in Vietnam during the specific period and currently has a medical condition listed in VA regulations as being caused by Agent Orange which began within the listed time periods, VA must service connect that condition. Conditions that are presumptively service-connected for herbicide exposure include chloracne, Type 2 diabetes (also known as Type II diabetes mellitus or adult-onset diabetes), Hodgkin's disease, Non-Hodgkin's lymphoma, B cell leukemia, Parkinson's disease, and ischemic heart disease. Other presumptive conditions are listed, so a Vietnam veteran with a health condition should review the entire list.

Just who is eligible for the herbicide presumption has been the topic of extensive debate and litigation. As it currently stands, having earned a Vietnam Service Medal is not enough to obtain the presumption. A veteran must show that he or she put "boots on the ground" in Vietnam or have been a "brown water" (inland waters) sailor to qualify. A single layover or shore leave is enough to receive the presumption. In addition, some veterans with service in Korea are also eligible for the presumption. For veterans with service in Thailand the key to claims for exposure are military duties that took the veteran out to and alongside the perimeter of bases where defoliants were acknowledged to have been used. Such duties include dog handling, security, and some maintenance activities.

On June 19th, 2015 the Federal Register published that Air Force Service members and Air Force Reservists who served during the period of 1969 through 1986 and whose service required that they regularly and repeatedly operate, maintain, or serve onboard C-123 aircraft that was exposed to Agent Orange are now eligible for VA disability compensation for presumptive conditions due to Agent Orange Exposure.

Another result of the Nehmer case is that if an individual was entitled to retroactive benefits as a result of the court orders but died prior to receiving such payment, VA must pay the entire amount of the retroactive payments to

the veteran's estate, regardless of any statutory limits on payment of benefits following a veteran's death. Veterans and surviving spouses, dependent children, and dependent parents of veterans with service in Vietnam who previously filed claims for conditions associated with herbicide exposure should carefully review current VA regulations to determine if they are eligible for retroactive benefits.

2. PTSD

Posttraumatic Stress Disorder (PTSD) is now included in a new chapter in DSM-5 on Trauma and Stressor Related Disorders. In the DSM-IV PTSD was addressed as an Anxiety disorder.

The diagnostic criteria for the manual's next edition identify the trigger to PTSD as exposure to actual or threatened death, serious injury or sexual violation. The exposure must result from one or more of the following scenarios, in which the individual:

- directly experiences the traumatic event;

- witnesses the traumatic event in person;

- learns that the traumatic event occurred to a close family member or close friend (with the actual or threatened death being either violent or accidental); or

- experiences first-hand repeated or extreme exposure to aversive details of the traumatic event (not through media, pictures, television or movies unless work-related).

The disturbance, regardless of its trigger, causes clinically significant distress or impairment in the individual's social interactions, capacity to work or other important areas of functioning. It is not the physiological result of another medical condition, medication, drugs or alcohol.

3. Military Sexual Trauma (MST)

Military sexual trauma, or MST, is the term used by the Department of Veterans Affairs (VA) to refer to experiences of sexual assault or repeated, threatening sexual harassment that a Veteran experienced during his or her military service.

The definition used by the VA comes from Federal law (Title 38 U.S. Code 1720D) and is "psychological trauma, which in the judgment of a VA mental health professional, resulted from a physical assault of a sexual nature, battery of a sexual nature, or sexual harassment which occurred while the Veteran was serving on active duty, active duty for training, or inactive duty training." Sexual harassment is further defined as "repeated, unsolicited verbal or physical contact of a sexual nature which is threatening in character."

Fortunately, people can recover from experiences of trauma, and VA has effective services to help Veterans do this. VA is strongly committed to ensuring that Veterans have access to the help they need in order to recover from MST.

Recognizing that many survivors of sexual trauma do not disclose their experiences unless asked directly, VA health care providers ask every Veteran whether he or she experienced MST. This is an important way of making sure Veterans know about the services available to them.

Services are designed to meet Veterans where they are at in their recovery, whether that is focusing on strategies for coping with challenging emotions and memories or, for Veterans who are ready, actually talking about their MST experiences in depth.

Nationwide, there are programs that offer specialized sexual trauma treatment in residential or inpatient settings. These are programs for Veterans who need more intense treatment and support. To accommodate Veterans who do not feel comfortable in mixed-gender treatment settings, some facilities have separate programs for men and women. All residential and inpatient MST programs have separate sleeping areas for men and women.

In addition to its treatment programming, VA also provides training to staff on issues related to MST, including a mandatory training on MST for all mental health and primary care providers. VA also engages in a range of outreach activities to Veterans and conducts monitoring of MST-related screening and treatment, in order to ensure that adequate services are available.

Military Sexual Trauma Details

MST includes any sexual activity where a Service member is involved against his or her will - he or she may have been pressured into sexual activities (for example, with threats of negative consequences for refusing to be sexually cooperative or with implied better treatment in exchange for sex), may have been unable to consent to sexual activities (for example, when intoxicated), or may have been physically forced into sexual activities. Other experiences that fall into the category of MST include:

-Unwanted sexual touching or grabbing

-Threatening, offensive remarks about a person's body or sexual activities

-Threatening and unwelcome sexual advances

The identity or characteristics of the perpetrator, whether the Service member was on or off duty at the time, and whether he or she was on or off base at the time do not matter. If these experiences occurred while an individual was on active duty or active duty for training, they are considered by VA to be MST.

CHAPTER 8 Duty TO OBTAIN

DUTY TO OBTAIN RECORDS

The VA is required to make "reasonable efforts" to obtain a claimant's military service records, VA medical records, and other pertinent federal records without being asked to do so. If a claimant requests assistance in obtaining records from private physicians and hospitals, VA is required to try to obtain those records as well. However, VA is not required to continue to request or wait for records if it determines that the records do not exist or further efforts to obtain the records would be futile. In addition, VA will not pay for obtaining private medical records.

As a practical matter, VA usually can obtain records from government agencies and the military without significant problems. There are situations, however, where VA does not properly request documents or the documents have been lost or destroyed by another agency. VA must inform a claimant of its failure to obtain relevant records. A claimant can and should submit his or her copy of relevant documents even if VA is technically responsible for obtaining the information because the lack of relevant information can result in denial of an otherwise valid claim.

"The Secretary shall make reasonable efforts to assist a claimant in obtaining evidence necessary to substantiate the claimant's claim for a benefit under a law administered by the Secretary." 38 U.S.C. § 5103A(a)(1). Gardner v. Shinseki, 22 Vet. App. 415, 421 (2009) ("Accordingly, the Secretary's duty to assist applies to all claimants, regardless of whether they have established veteran status."). VA is statutorily required to "make as many requests as are necessary" to obtain a veteran's relevant service records in the custody of a Federal department or agency. 38 C.F.R. § 3.159(c) (2); see Moore v. Shinseki, 555 F.3d 1369, 1374 (Fed. Cir. 2009); see also Murincsak v. Derwinski, 2 Vet. App. 363, 373 (1992) ("There is a continuing obligation upon the VA to assist the veteran in developing the facts of his claim throughout the entire administrative adjudication.").

Upon receipt of a complete or substantially complete application for benefits and prior to an initial unfavorable decision on a claim by an agency of original jurisdiction, the Secretary is required to inform the claimant of the information and evidence not of record that:

(1) is necessary to substantiate the claim,

(2) the Secretary will seek to obtain, if any, and

(3) the claimant is expected to provide, if any, and to request that the claimant provide any evidence in his possession that pertains to the claim.

See 38 U.S.C. § 5103(a); Pelegrini v. Principi, 18 Vet. App. 112, 119, 121 (2004); Quartuccio v. Principi, 16 Vet. App. 183, 187 (2002); 38 C.F.R. § 3.159(b). This duty includes making "reasonable efforts to obtain relevant records (including private records) that the claimant adequately identifies to the Secretary and authorizes the Secretary to obtain." 38 U.S.C. § 5103A(b)(1). If the Secretary is unable to obtain all of the records sought, the Secretary must provide notice to the claimant that "identif[ies] the records that the Secretary was unable to obtain," "briefly explain[s] the efforts that the Secretary made to obtain those records," and "describe[s] any further action to be taken by the Secretary with respect to the claim." 38 U.S.C. § 5103A(b)(2). These requirements also apply to private documents.

The "duty to assist in the development and adjudication of a claim is not a one-way street." Wamhoff v. Brown, 8 Vet. App. 517, 522 (1996). VA's duty to assist includes making "reasonable efforts to assist a claimant in obtaining evidence necessary to substantiate the claimant's claim for a benefit." 38 U.S.C. §§ 5103A (a)(1), (b); cf. The Board's determination whether VA fulfilled its duty to assist generally is a finding of fact that the Court reviews under the "clearly erroneous" standard of review. See Nolen v. Gober, 14 Vet. App. 183, 184 (2000); Gilbert v. Derwinski, 1 Vet. App. 49, 52 (1990).

DUTY TO OBTAIN LOST OR MISSING RECORDS

VA's duty in cases involving lost records is to seek out alternative sources for obtaining the lost records. Cromer v. Nicholson, 455 F.3d 1346, 1351 (Fed. Cir. 2006). Pursuant to 38 U.S.C. section 5103A, the Secretary is required to "make reasonable efforts to assist a claimant in obtaining evidence necessary to substantiate the claimant's claim for benefits." 38 U.S.C. §§ 5103A (a), (b). Where a claimant's records are lost or destroyed, VA has a "heightened" duty to assist the claimant that includes advising him that his records were lost, advising him to submit alternative forms of evidence to support his claim, and assisting him in obtaining his alternative evidence. Washington v. Nicholson, 19 Vet. App. 362, 370 (2005); Dixon v. Derwinski, 3 Vet. App. 261, 263 (1992).

However, the Court cannot grant an appellant's claim solely because his records were lost because that remedy "would amount to a judicial amendment of the statutory duty to assist-a measure beyond the power of this court." Id. at 1351. A veteran bears the burden of showing error on this issue. See Hilkert v. West, 12 Vet. App. 145, 151 (1999) (holding that the appellant bears the burden of demonstrating error); Berger v. Brown, 10 Vet. App. 166, 169 (1997) (holding that an appellant "always bears the burden of persuasion on appeals to this Court").

When medical records are lost, it warrants a heightened duty by the Secretary and the Board to assist and explain the Board's findings. See Vazquez-Flores, supra; see also Cromer v. Nicolson, 455 F.3d 1346, 1351 (Fed. Cir. 2006) ("[I]n cases involving lost records, the Board has a heightened duty to explain its findings."); Daye v. Nicholson, 20 Vet. App. 512, 515 (2006) (where appellant's records not available, the duty to assist and fully explain reasons and bases is heightened); Stegall, supra; see also Russo v. Brown, 9 Vet. App. 46, 51 (1996) (holding that the Court's case law establishes a "heightened duty" to assist when the appellant's medical records have been lost or destroyed); Cuevas v. Principi, 3 Vet. App. 542, 548 (1992) (holding that the Board's duty to assist a claimant in developing his claim is heightened in cases in which the appellant's SMRs are lost or destroyed "and includes the obligation to search for alternate medical records"); Moore v. Derwinski, 1 Vet. App. 401, 406 (1991) (holding that VA's duty to assist is "particularly great in light of the unavailability of the veteran's exit examination and full Army medical records").

DUTY TO PROVIDE MEDICAL EXAMINATION

VA is required to schedule a compensation and pension (C&P) examination for a claimant at the nearest VA medical center unless there is a good reason for not doing so, such as when an expert is required that is not available at the nearest facility or the examination is with a VA medical contractor. VA, however, does not have to provide a medical examination in all cases. The standard for providing a medical examination is usually not difficult to meet. VA, however, can refuse to provide a VA medical examination unless there is some reasonable possibility that an examination will provide information that could be useful in deciding the claim.

In general, to obtain a C&P examination a claimant needs to show a current medical condition, some evidence of potential connection to service, and that available medical evidence is not sufficient to allow a decision on the claim. In other words, the claimant must first provide some reason for VA to believe that a medical examination would be helpful in resolving the claim. A claimant's own statement that his or her symptoms have continued since service or a previous medical examination report can be enough of a reason.

Should VA schedule a medical examination, a claimant has a duty to report for the examination. In most cases, if the claimant does not show up for an examination, the claim(s) associated with that examination can be denied without further development. There are some reasons for failing to show for a scheduled examination, such as illness or urgent family emergency that can be excused. Even so, claimants should make every effort to reschedule an examination in advance to avoid problems.

As part of his duty to assist, the Secretary must "make reasonable efforts to assist a claimant in obtaining evidence necessary to substantiate the claimant's claim for a benefit" including a medical examination. 38 U.S.C. § 5103A (a) (1). The Secretary must provide a medical examination or obtain a medical opinion "when such an examination or opinion is necessary to make a decision on the claim." 38 U.S.C. § 5103A (d)(1). VA must provide a medical opinion or examination if the information and evidence of record does not contain sufficiently competent medical evidence to decide the claim, but there is:

(1) Competent evidence of a current disability or persistent or recurrent symptoms of a disability;

(2) Evidence establishing that an event, injury, or disease occurred in service or establishing certain diseases manifesting during an applicable presumptive period for which the claimant qualifies; and

(3) An indication that the disability or persistent or recurrent symptoms of a disability may be associated with the veteran's service or with another service-connected disability. 38 C.F.R. § 3.159(c)(4)(i). The requirement that the evidence indicate that a condition "may be associated" with service establishes a "low threshold."

When deciding whether an examination is necessary, the Secretary shall consider the evidence of record, "taking into consideration all information and lay or medical evidence (including statements of the claimant)." 38 U.S.C. §

5103A(d)(2). "The Board's ultimate conclusion that a medical examination is not necessarily pursuant to section 5103A(d)(2) is reviewed under the 'arbitrary, capricious, an abuse of discretion, or otherwise not in accordance with law' standard of review." McLendon, 20 Vet. App. at 81.

Generally, section 5103A notice must be given on "all five elements of a claim for service connection," which include:

(1) Veteran status

(2) Existence of disability

(3) Service connection of disability

(4) Degree of disability

(5) Effective date of disability.

DUTY TO IDENTIFY INFERRED CLAIMS

Once VA has gathered all the reasonably obtainable information, including information submitted by the claimant, VA must decide whether or not to grant an award of benefits. In making that decision, VA must consider three other duties owed to the claimant: (1) duty to identify inferred claims, (2) duty to consider all reasonable legal theories, and (3) duty to maximize benefits. In other words, VA has several duties to apply the rules to the facts in a case in whatever way provides the most generous benefits allowed by the law.

These duties do not mean that VA has to look at every possible combination of rules and facts that may be even remotely possible. VA, however, has to review the entire record and apply the applicable provisions of law that are reasonably raised by the evidence. In addition, whether or not new claims are identified, VA must also review the diagnostic codes for the code or combination of codes that results in the highest benefit for the claimant.

Overall, in creating the duty to assist Congress recognized that VA raters are better trained and more experienced with the rules for obtaining benefits than the average claimant. VA must look for claims and grant awards based on all the evidence in the C-file whether or not the claimant asked for the specific benefit. This is a very good reason for claimants to provide as much information as possible when submitting applications or responding to VA requests.

CHAPTER 9 MISCELANOUS KNOWLEDGE

Nexus Letter

A "nexus letter" is a document prepared for a claimant by a medical professional that explicitly connects an in-service event to the current medical condition for which a claimant is seeking compensation. A claimant is not required to submit a nexus letter, but such a letter can make the difference between an award and a denial. A nexus letter can be submitted with an initial application, during claim development, or after an adverse C&P exam. Submitting a properly worded nexus letter as early as possible in the process, however, is good practice.

A nexus letter is especially important in cases where a claimant has not submitted any medical evidence and a C&P examiner concludes that there is no connection between a claimant's condition and military service. Without a nexus letter, the claim will be denied. Even when a claimant supplies supporting medical evidence with an application, VA raters can and often do choose the opinion of the VA examiner over a private physician's opinion for many reasons. In such a case, a "nexus letter" from a private physician is necessary to respond to the C&P examiner's conclusion.

One reason for raters favoring VA examiner's conclusions regarding a nexus when there are conflicting or unclear medical opinions is that VA examiners are more familiar with the terms that raters look for when deciding a claim. As described above, VA regulations require only that it be "at least as likely as not" that a condition be related to service for an award. This means that the likelihood of service connection is equal to or greater than 50% (a 50/50 chance or better).

Most medical professionals, however, are not familiar with the VA system or the VA concept of "at least as likely as not." Physicians are generally familiar with the concept of "medical certainty," which is a much higher standard than that required by VA. As a result, private physicians may apply the wrong standard if the VA terms are not explained to them. Even then, a private physician may be reluctant to state a conclusion regarding nexus and, if they do, may qualify their conclusion with terms such as "may," "could," "suggests," or "possibly." VA will often point to such qualifying terms as not meeting the legal standard for establishing a nexus, although the physician actually believed that the condition was more than 50% likely service connected.

To prevent such misunderstandings, a claimant should make sure that the medical professional asked to provide a nexus letter understands the importance of the letter and of using the VA "magic words" to correctly state the physician's medical opinion. The terms "more likely than not" (meaning greater than 50% likelihood of a connection) and "at least as likely as not" (meaning equal to or greater than 50% likelihood of a connection) are important to use so that VA will have to recognize the nexus letter as supporting service-connection. Any other terms may be misunderstood or misconstrued by VA into something not supporting service-connection. Bringing the relevant C&P Examination Worksheet to the examination or providing it to the medical professional may be helpful.

The Court has stated that "when a nexus between a current disability and an in-service event is 'indicated,' there must be a medical opinion that provides some nonspeculative determination as to the degree of likelihood that a disability was caused by an in-service disease or incident to constitute sufficient medical evidence on which the Board can render a decision with regard to nexus." McLendon v. Nicholson, 20 Vet. App. 79, 85 (2006) (emphasis added). The Court has also noted that medical evidence that is too speculative to establish nexus is also insufficient to establish a lack of nexus; a VA medical examination must be undertaken to resolve the nexus issue. Id. (citing Forshey v. Principi, 284 F.3d 1335, 1363 (Fed. Cir. 2002) (Mayer, C.J., and Newman, J., dissenting) ("The absence of actual evidence is not substantive 'negative evidence'")). Jones v. Shinseki, 23 Vet. App. 382, 387-88 (2010).

If the Board finds his or her testimony credible, a claimant does not need competent medical evidence to substantiate his or her claim. See Savage v. Gober, 10 Vet. App. 488, 495–96 (1997) (holding that, per 38 C.F.R. section 3.303(b), medical evidence of nexus is not required for benefits if the veteran demonstrates continuity of symptoms between his present disability and service); see also Davidson v. Shinseki, 581 F.3d 1313, 1316 (Fed. Cir. 2009). Arneson v. Shinseki, 24 Vet. App. 379, 388 (2011).

Effective Date

The determination of the effective date for an original claim or a reopened claim is governed by 38 U.S.C. section 5110(a), which provides: "Unless specifically provided otherwise in this chapter, the effective date of an award based on an original claim [or] a claim reopened after final adjudication . . . shall be fixed in accordance with the facts found, but shall not be earlier than the date of receipt of application therefor." The implementing regulation similarly states that the effective date shall be the date of receipt of the claim or the date entitlement arose, whichever is later, unless the claim is received within one year after separation from service. See 38 C.F.R. § 3.400. "Generally, effective dates of compensation awards are attached to the date of receipt of the application for benefits, and no earlier." Sharp v. Shinseki, 23 Vet. App. 267, 273 (2009) (citing 38 U.S.C. § 5110(a)). Significantly, "the effective date of an award of service connection is not based on the date of the earliest medical evidence demonstrating a causal connection, but on the date that the application upon which service connection was eventually awarded was filed with VA." Lalonde v. West, 12 Vet. App. 377, 382 (1999); see Brannon v. West, 12 Vet. App. 32, 35 (1998) (the "mere presence of medical evidence does not establish the intent on the part of a veteran to seek service connection for a condition.").

The effective date may also be the date on which entitlement to the benefit arose, if later than the date of the claim. 38 C.F.R. § 3.400(o). A challenge to a decision assigning an effective date with which a claimant disagrees may be made through a direct appeal of the decision, commencing with the timely filing of a Notice of Disagreement. 38 U.S.C. § 7105. The NOD must be in writing and filed within one year "from the date of mailing of notice of the result of initial review or determination." 38 U.S.C. § 7105(b)(1). Rowell v. Principi, 4 Vet. App. 9, 17 (1993); Cuevas v. Principi, 3 Vet. App. 542, 546 (1992). Alternatively, if the decision assigning an effective date has become final, a claimant may only pursue one of the statutory exceptions to challenge the finality of that decision. See DiCarlo v. Nicholson, 20 Vet. App. 52, 56-57 (2006) (discussing the types of collateral attack authorized to challenge a final decision by the Secretary); see also Cook v. Principi, 318 F.3d 1334, 1339 (Fed. Cir. 2002) (en banc) (same).

However, in Rudd v. Nicholson, 20 Vet. App. 296, 299 (2006), the Court held that claimants may not properly file, and VA has no authority to adjudicate, a freestanding earlier-effective-date claim in an attempt to overcome the finality of an unappealed RO decision. The Court reasoned that to allow such claims would vitiate the rule of finality. Id. Although there are numerous exceptions to the rule of finality and application of res judicata within the VA adjudication system, a freestanding claim for an earlier effective date is not one of the recognized statutory exceptions to finality. See DeLisio v. Shinseki, 25 Vet. App. 45, 51 ("[A]n effective date generally can be no earlier than the date of the claim."); Canady v. Nicholson, 20 Vet. App. 393, 398 (2006) (holding that a "proper effective date is a finding of fact" reviewed under the "clearly erroneous" standard).

A claimant may establish an effective date earlier than the date of the claim if the claimant is able to show an increase in disability in the one-year period preceding the claim. Hart v. Mansfield, 21 Vet. App. 505, 509 (2007) ("When a claim for an increased rating is granted, the effective date assigned may be up to one year prior to the date that the application for increase was received if it is factually ascertainable that an increase in disability had occurred within that timeframe."); Dalton v. Nicholson, 21 Vet. App. 23, 34 (2007) ("Board is required to search the record to determine whether it is factually ascertainable that in the one year prior to the application there was an increase in disability."); Harper v. Brown, 10 Vet. App. 125, 126-27 (1997) (noting that the general rule applies unless it is factually ascertainable that the increase occurred within the year preceding the filing of the claim); see also Scott v. Brown, 7 Vet. App. 184, 189 (1994) (under the terms of section 5110(b)(2), the effective date is either the date of the claim or "some date in the preceding year if it were ascertainable that the disability had increased in severity during that time").

In other words, the actual increase in disability must have occurred during the one-year period immediately preceding the date of the claim; any evidence demonstrating an increase earlier than the one-year period is not a basis for an effective date earlier than the date of the claim. The Board's determination of the proper effective date for an award of VA benefits is a finding of fact reviewed under the "clearly erroneous" standard of review set forth in 38 U.S.C. § 7261(a)(4).

There are only two ways to establish an earlier effective date after a decision has become final: (1) by establishing a "Clear and Unmistakable Error" was made or (2) by submitting official service department records that existed, but were not considered, in a decision. See 38 U.S.C. §§ 5109A, 7111; 38 C.F.R. §§ 3.156(c); 20.1403. As discussed elsewhere in this Knowledge Book, CUE is a "very specific and rare kind of error" that has special pleading requirements. Section 3.156(c), however, is fairly straightforward. If VA or a claimant discovers a service department record, such as a service record, service medical record, or unit report or log, and it is relevant to a previous decision, VA must reconsider that decision. If reconsideration of the claim with the newly found record results in an award, the effective date of that award is the date that the originally denied claim was submitted, no matter how far back. 38 C.F.R. § 3.156(c)(3).

The St. Louis Fire

In 1973 there was a fire at the National Personnel Records Center ("NPRC") in St. Louis. The NPRC is an official repository for records of military veterans who served in the United States Army, Navy, Air Force, Marine Corps, and Coast Guard. This event is important to many veterans because a large number of military service records were destroyed. The "fire" has become something of an urban legend because VA sometimes cites it as reason for not obtaining a veteran's service records, sometimes even when the veteran left service after the fire occurred. According to a VA "Fact Sheet," the fire destroyed about 80% of Army records for persons discharged between November 1912 and January 1960 and about 75% of Air Force records for persons discharged between September 1947 and January 1964. Because of poor recordkeeping and loaning of records, it is not possible to say for sure exactly which records were destroyed within these groups.

No other records were lost in the fire. VA itself has stated that records for veterans who left service after 1964 were not affected and that only Army and Air

Force records were involved (no Navy records were affected). Clearly, records for veterans who left service after 1973 could not have been destroyed in a 1973 file. As a result, any time the "fire" is cited as a reason for VA not locating service records, veterans should take the time to determine if the record could have been affected and, if not, challenge the VA's conclusion.

Clear and Unmistakable Error

A decision that has become final may not be reversed or revised in the absence of a showing of CUE. 38 U.S.C. § 7111(a). CUE "is a very specific and rare kind of error . . . that when called to the attention of later reviewers compels the conclusion, to which reasonable minds could not differ, that the result would have been manifestly different but for the error." 38 C.F.R. § 20.1403(a).

The Court has no jurisdiction to consider a CUE claim it in the first instance. 38 U.S.C. § 7252(a); Andrea v. Principi, 301 F.3d 1354, 1361 (Fed. Cir. 2002) (holding that "each 'specific' assertion of CUE constitutes a claim that must be the subject of a decision by the [Board] before the Veteran's Court can exercise jurisdiction over it"); Russell v. Principi, 3 Vet. App. 310, 315 (1992) (en banc) (noting that "[t]he necessary jurisdictional 'hook' for this Court to act is a decision of the [Board] on the specific issue of 'clear and unmistakable error'").VA law allows a veteran – at any time – to request that a decision be reviewed and corrected if VA committed a "clear and unmistakable error" (often called a "CUE"). This is a very powerful right. Unfortunately, it is also a widely misunderstood and a misapplied right. A true CUE is not common and is a difficult claim to win.

A CUE is a special type of error and a claim for revision of a previous denial on the basis of CUE can be filed at any time, even years or decades after the claim was decided or the appeal denied.

(1) Claim must be a "closed claim" also known as a "final decision" for a CUE review. The final decision must be from the VARO, Veterans Administration Regional Office, or the BVA, Board of Veterans Appeals and was never appealed, and

(2) Either the correct facts were not before the adjudicator or the statutory or regulatory provisions in existence at the time were incorrectly applied; and

(3) The error is "undebatable;" and

(4) The error must make a difference in the outcome. In other words, a CUE is not a disagreement with a decision or an argument that VA got it wrong.

When CUE does occur and a claim is granted, the usual rules for setting the effective date of an award is by-passed. The effective date of a CUE claim goes back all the way to the filing date of the claim with the CUE. This can result in huge awards of retroactive benefits.

Because a claim for CUE is a review of an already "closed claim" also known as "final decision claim", special rules apply:

The "duty to assist" does not apply. This means that VA does not help a claimant with a CUE claim.

A CUE claim must contain specific and detailed statements regarding the error:

How that error affected the decision, and

Why the decision would be different (more favorable to the claimant) if the error is corrected. Merely stating that CUE occurred or general statements similar to those in a benefits claim are not enough. For example: a decision awarding benefits based on a single gunshot wound when the veteran had two gunshot wounds is a CUE. A CUE claim asserting that a gunshot wound was more painful than VA concluded is clearly not a CUE.

CUE WARNING:

A veteran can only claim CUE one time for each decision. This means that if a claimant files a CUE claim and the VA finds that the claim does not contain the required level of detail, that CUE claim is lost forever. For this reason, claimants who believe that they have a possible CUE claim are strongly urged to seek advice from a VSO, registered agent, or experienced attorney.

Errors that cannot constitute CUE, pursuant to 38 C.F.R. sections 20.1403(d) and (e), include:

(1)   A changed diagnosis, where a "new medical diagnosis . . . 'corrects' an earlier diagnosis considered in a Board decision;"

(2) VA's failure to comply with the duty to assist;

(3) A "disagreement as to how the facts were weighed;" and

(4) A subsequent change in interpretation of the statute or regulation that was applied in the Board decision.

§ 20.1403 Rule 1403. What constitutes clear and unmistakable error; what does not.

(a) General. Clear and unmistakable error is a very specific and rare kind of error. It is the kind of error, of fact or of law, that when called to the attention of later reviewers compels the conclusion, to which reasonable minds could not differ, that the result would have been manifestly different but for the error. Generally, either the correct facts, as they were known at the time, were not before the Board, or the statutory and regulatory provisions extant at the time were incorrectly applied.

(b) Record to be reviewed—

(1) General. Review for clear and unmistakable error in a prior Board decision must be based on the record and the law that existed when that decision was made.

(2) Special rule for Board decisions issued on or after July 21, 1992. For a Board decision issued on or after July 21, 1992, the record that existed when that decision was made includes relevant documents possessed by the Department of Veterans Affairs not later than 90 days before such record was transferred to the Board for review in reaching that decision, provided that the documents could reasonably be expected to be part of the record.

(c) Errors that constitute clear and unmistakable error. To warrant revision of a Board decision on the grounds of clear and unmistakable error, there must have been an error in the Board's adjudication of the appeal which, had it not been made, would have manifestly changed the outcome when it was made. If it is not absolutely clear that a different result would have ensued, the error complained of cannot be clear and unmistakable.

(d) Examples of situations that are not clear and unmistakable error—

(1) Changed diagnosis. A new medical diagnosis that "corrects" an earlier diagnosis considered in a Board decision.

(2) Duty to assist. The Secretary's failure to fulfill the duty to assist.

(3) Evaluation of evidence. A disagreement as to how the facts were weighed or evaluated.

(e) Change in interpretation. Clear and unmistakable error does not include the otherwise correct application of a statute or regulation where, subsequent to the Board decision challenged, there has been a change in the interpretation of the statute or regulation.

(Authority: 38 U.S.C. 501(a), 7111)

The Fully Developed Claim Is an Effective and Timely Procedure for Getting Results

The concept behind a Fully Developed Claim is that you will give the Regional Office every scrap of relevant and probative evidence you can get your hands on to make your case. You will provide this information up front when you make your formal application by filling out the appropriate benefit forms and including all of your evidence with it. The goal is for all of the evidence that you assemble to be sufficient enough for the Regional Office development team to pass on to the rating activity for a final decision. This Fully Developed Claim concept could get you a decision within a matter of a few months instead of the typical 8 to 18 months that it takes by simply applying and waiting for VA to assist you in developing your evidence.

Elements of the Fully Developed Claim Process for Disability Compensation

1. Decide Whether the Condition Warrants Making a Claim
2. Always Submit an "Intent to File", VBA Form 21-0966
3. Obtain Your Discharge and Your Own Service Treatment Records STRs)
4. Obtain Your Own Private Medical Records
5. Obtain Disability Evaluations from Private Clinicians Where Possible
6. Have Your Doctors/Specialists Provide Opinion Letters If Needed

7. Produce Lay Statements

8. Locate Records to Establish Duty Assignments Where Applicable

9. Make Sure Your Evidence Is Convincing

10. Understand the Claim Forms and the Forms for Obtaining Records

11. Fill out the "Fully Developed Claim" Form for the Claimed Benefit

12. Double Check Everything and Include Necessary Documentation

13. Arrange for Representation and Third-Party Help If Needed

14. Provide a Cover Letter to Service Representatives

15. Submit the Claim to the Scanning Center

16. Understand the Acknowledgment from Your Veterans Service Center

17. Use VA Form 21-4138 for Purposes of Correspondence on the Claim

18. Expect Scheduling of a Compensation and Pension Examination

19. What to Do If the Claimant Dies before the Claim Is Adjudicated

KEY ACTS AND STATUTES

Veterans' Judicial Review Act of 1988 ("VJRA")

Established the Court of Appeals for Veterans Claims (originally named the "Court of Veterans Appeals") and authorized judicial review of VA benefits decisions for the first time.

Veterans Claims Assistance Act of 2000 ("VCAA")

Eliminated the requirement that a claimant must first submit enough evidence to make his or her claim "well grounded" before VA would process a claim and added the requirement for VA to make "reasonable efforts to assist a claimant in obtaining evidence necessary to substantiate the claimant's claim" which is the "duty to assist."

Chapter 10 Appeals Process

VA Form 20-0995 Supplemental Claim Form is one of several newer forms in a decision review process that replaced the legacy process in 2019. If you disagree with a VA decision that was dated on or after February 19, 2019, you can now choose from three decision review options or "lanes" **(Supplemental Claim, Higher-Level Review, or Board Appeal)** to continue your case.

A SUPPLEMENTAL CLAIM is a new review of an issue(s) previously decided by the Department of Veterans Affairs (VA) based on submission of new and relevant evidence.

Section 1 – Claimant's Identifying Information

This section requires basic information: full name, Social Security Number, date of birth, current mailing address, telephone number, and benefit type (e.g., compensation, pension/survivors' benefits, etc.).

In this section you're also asked to check a box regarding what type of benefit you're appealing. You can only check one, so if you plan to appeal decisions for multiple types of benefits, complete separate forms for each benefit type.

Section 2 – Issue(s) for Supplemental Claim

In this section, list each issue that you are wanting the VA to reopen and adjudicate. Each specific issue must be cited along with the date of the VA decision notice in which it was originally either denied or partially granted (for example, if you received a decision granting you a 70 percent disability rating for a condition, but you feel that you are entitled to a 100% rating).

This section also includes a checkbox to indicate if you're opting into the new appeals system following a Statement of the Case (SOC) or Supplemental Statement of the Case (SSOC) from the legacy (former) appeals system. If you had a claim in the legacy system, checking that box withdraws all eligible appeal issues listed on the form from the legacy system and affirms your participation in the new system. (NOTE: if you take this option, it may alter the effective date of your claim.)

Section 3 – New and Relevant Evidence

This section addresses the need for new and relevant evidence for Supplemental Claims via VA-0995 and is used if you want the VA to obtain records on your behalf. Complete columns 15A and 15B with name, location, and dates of the records you want retrieved. This will allow the VA to retrieve public records on your behalf; if you want the VA to gather evidence from a private provider, you must fill out and sign **VA Form 21-4142 (PDF)** and include it with your Supplemental Claim form (VA Form 20-0995).

Section 4 —5103—Notice Acknowledgement

If you select "NO" in this section, the claim will not be adjudicated for 30 days, and the VA will mail you a notice of that fact. Select "YES" and click on the Notice Acknowledgement link to view the notice so your Supplemental Claim is not delayed.

Section 4 – Certification and Signature

Sign and date the form to authorize your Supplemental Claim request. You're signifying that the information on your 20-0995 form is true and correct.

VA FORM 0996 Higher-Level Review

A Higher-Level Review is a new review of an issue(s) previously decided by the Department of Veterans Affairs (VA) **based on the evidence of record at the time VA issued notice of the prior decision. The Higher-Level Reviewer will not consider any evidence received after the notification date of the prior decision.**

A Higher-Level Review may not be requested for the review of a Higher-Level Review decision or a Board of Veterans' Appeals decision. This form must be submitted to VA WITHIN ONE YEAR OF THE DATE VA PROVIDED NOTICE OF OUR DECISION.

To begin the appeals process, a veteran must fill out and turn in the Decision Review Request: Higher Level Review form **(VA Form 20-0996).** This can be submitted via mail, Fax, or by turning it indirectly at the nearest VA facility.

Once your form is submitted, you have several options. You can wait for the VA to request more information or schedule exams for you. You can request a conference call with your reviewer to speak with them about any errors you identified on your original claim and reasons why you think your decision should be rendered differently.

Any appeal for Higher Level Review (or HLR) from a veteran will be assigned a Decision Review Officer. This is a senior adjudicator who will take a fresh look at the previous VA decision. These officers are more experienced than those who first reviewed the claim and are generally based in a different location. This initial review will only consider the evidence presented initially in the claim. This is called a de novo review.

The officer then may overturn the decision if they disagree with the original decision. They may also find errors made in the assessment. If an error is encountered, they can request a correction.

Veterans may not appeal a Board decision to a Higher-Level Review or request a Higher-Level Review of the HLR you received. You also cannot appeal to the Board consecutively.

If the Board issues a decision you disagree with, you may continue with a Supplemental Claim or appeal to the Court of Appeals for Veterans Claims (or CAVC).

Appeals to the Board are officially supposed to be determined within one year. Also, so long as the appeal has remained active, there will be no change to your potential effective date for benefits.

Decision Review Request: Board Appeal (VA Form 10182)

If you have received a decision from a local VA office or a higher-level adjudicator with which you disagree, and you would like one or more issues to be decided by a Veterans Law Judge, you must fill out and submit a Notice of Disagreement. You can choose to appeal all or only some of the issues previously decided, however, ONLY those issues that you list on your Notice of Disagreement will be considered on appeal.

If you select a Board Appeal, you have 3 options. We encourage you to work with your representative to decide which of the following options is best for you.

Option 1: Request a Direct Review

A Veterans Law Judge will review your appeal based on evidence already submitted. You can't submit evidence and can't have a hearing.

The Direct Review option will take about one year for the Board to complete.

Option 2: Submit more evidence

You can submit more evidence for a Veterans Law Judge to review. You must submit this evidence within 90 days of the date we receive your Decision Review Request: Board Appeal **(VA Form 10182).**

The evidence submission option will take more than one year for the Board to complete.

Option 3: Request a hearing

You can request a hearing with a Veterans Law Judge. You can choose to add new and relevant evidence, either at the hearing or within 90 days after the hearing. Adding evidence is optional. Your hearing will be transcribed and added to your appeal file.

You can choose from 3 different ways to speak with the Veterans Law Judge:

- Virtual hearing from your home
- Videoconference hearing at a VA location near you
- In-person hearing at the Board in Washington, D.C.

The hearing request option will take more than one year for the Board to complete.

APPENDIX

Your DD-214

The Department of Defense issues Form 214 to separating members of the military. The form is essential evidence in most determinations of benefits eligibility. Modern DD 214's will list the veteran's Characterization of Service in Block 24. The Reason for Separation will be listed in Block 28.

Veterans are issued both redacted and unredacted copies of their DD 214. The purpose of the redacted copy (sometimes called "Member Copy 1") is to allow the veteran to prove military service without disclosing discharge information. Advocates will want an unredacted copy of the DD 214 that includes Characterization of Service, Reason for Separation, and Authority for Separation.

National Guard servicemembers without federal "active" service will receive a National Guard Bureau Form 22 ("NGB 22") instead or in addition to a DD214 for any federal service.

How Do I Get My DD-214?

Most veterans and their next-of-kin can obtain free copies of their DD Form 214 (Report of Separation) and other records several ways:

Archive's eVetRecs online military records request system.   Through this system, located at http://www.archives.gov/veterans/evetrecs/ Use our eVetRecs system to create your request

Complete and submit the electronic application you must print off and sign the application and mail it or fax it to the Archives within 30 days. If your signature is not received within 30 days your request will automatically be deleted from the Archive's request system. Make sure to make an additional copy for your records as well.

If you do not have internet access you can also make a request by mail or by fax. Although it is not mandatory it is strongly suggested you make your request on a Standard Form (SF) 180. A SF 180 is available for download at http://www.archives.gov/research/order/standard-form-180.pdf. If you are unable to obtain an electronic copy of a SF 180 you can request a copy be mailed to you by mailing your request to:

National Personnel Records Center

9700 Page Avenue

St. Louis, Missouri 63132

Fax a letter or Standard Form 180 to: 314-801-9195

The Center will respond in writing by U.S. Mail.

ACRONYMS AND DEFINITIONS

The following is a sampling of some of the acronyms that a claimant or appellant may see in various VA records and documents.

1151 Claim A claim for benefits under 38 U.S.C. Section 1151 as a result of injury caused by VA treatment or rehabilitation services similar to a medical malpractice claim.

Appellant   The party in an appeal who is challenging the decision on appeal. At the Board and the Court, the claimant seeking benefits (veteran or dependent) is always the Appellant.

Appellee   The party in an appeal who is defending the decision on appeal. In the Veterans Court, the VA Secretary is always the Appellee.

Board The Board of Veterans' Appeals. The Board is the organization within VA that reviews appeals of unfavorable initial rating decisions.

BVA   An acronym for the Board of Veterans' Appeals.

C-file Claims file. VA creates a hard copy paper file for each claimant that contains all the documents related to that claimant since the first application for benefits. C-files can contain thousands of pages of documents and must be physically shipped between offices when claims are reviewed by different VA groups or the Veterans Court.

CAVC The Unites States Court of Appeals for Veterans Claims. The appellate court to which claimants can appeal adverse Board decisions. Also known as the "Court," "CAVC," or "Veterans Court."

Claim Number   Each claimant is assigned an unique VA claim number that VA uses to identify that claimant for life. Claimants should put their claim number on each document and correspondence sent to VA.

Compensation   A monetary benefit awarded based on the degree of disability caused by a service-connected condition.

DIC Dependency & Indemnity Compensation. A benefit awarded to surviving spouses and qualifying dependents and dependent parents when a service-connected condition is a cause of a veteran's death.

DRO Decision Review Officer. Usually an experienced member of a regional office rating team who reviews a rating decision at the request of the claimant after an initial denial. DRO review is optional and cannot change decisions favorable to a claimant except for fraud or similar issues.

DVA The Department of Veterans Affairs. A technically more accurate acronym than "VA," although not as widely used.

EFT Electronic Fund Transfer

Federal Circuit the United States Court of Appeals for the Federal Circuit. The federal appellate court to which claimants and VA can appeal Court decisions.

Form 9 The VA form that must be submitted after receipt of a Statement of the Case to perfect an appeal to the Board of Veterans' Appeals.

NOD Notice of Disagreement. Claimants must file a written NOD within one year of receiving a rating decision to be able to appeal that decision.

Pension A VA benefit based on financial need available to fully disabled veterans and unemployed veterans over age 65 who served during a time of war.

Presumption A legal term meaning that no evidence of a nexus between a current medical condition and an in-service occurrence is required. A claimant currently suffering from a "presumptive condition" only needs to establish he or she experienced the specified in-service event to be awarded service connection.

PTSD Post-Traumatic Stress Disorder.

Rating Decision The initial VA decision on a claim which either grants or denies an award. In some cases, VA may "continue" a claim for further development.

Rating Schedule The table of medical conditions and disabilities established by law that VA raters use to determine the degree of disability for compensation purposes.

Remand Return of a decision to the organization that made it for additional review and revision. For most claimants, the Board remands decisions to the originating regional office or the AMC. The Court remands Board decisions to the Board.

Secretary The Secretary of Veterans Affairs. The Cabinet officer who is the administrative head of VA.

Service Connection A requirement that a claimant for VA compensation must (1) have a current medical condition; (2) identify an event or condition during military service; and (3) establish a nexus or connection between the medical condition and the in-service event or condition. Without establishing service connection, VA will not award compensation benefits.

SMC Special Monthly Compensation. Additional compensation available to the most seriously disabled veterans for anatomical loss of limbs or loss of use of body parts, aid and attendance, and other special needs.

SOC Statement of the Case. A document that VA must prepare and provide to a claimant who has submitted a timely Notice of Disagreement. The purpose of an SOC is to identify the facts and law VA used to reach the decision(s) with which the claimant disagrees.

TDIU Total Disability based on Individual Unemployability. A special rating that considers whether a claimant who does not meet the rating schedule requirements for 100% disability is still unable to work in a substantially gainful occupation. A TDIU award pays benefits at the 100% scheduler rate even though the actual rating percentage is less than 100%.

VA The most commonly used acronym for the Department of Veterans Affairs.

Veterans Court Another common name for the United States Court of Appeals for Veterans Claims. See also CAVC.

V L J Veterans Law Judge. A member of the Board of Veterans' Appeals who hears appeals from claimants who disagree with a rating decision.

VONAPP Veterans Online Application. A VA website for electronically applying for VA benefits. https://www.ebenefits.va.gov/ebenefits-portal/ebenefits.portal?_nfpb=true&_nfxr=false&_pageLabel=Vonapp

2. ACRONYMS & TERMS USED IN VA BENEFITS CLAIMS & APPEALS

Much like the Department of Defense (DOD), the United States Department of Veterans Affairs (VA) uses many acronyms in the handling of claims and appeals for VA benefits. The following is a sampling of some of the acronyms that a claimant or appellant may see in various military and VA records and documents.

10-10EZ   VA Form 10-10EZ, Application for Health Benefits

10-10EZR   VA Form 10-10EZR, Health Benefits Renewal Form

10-10EC   VA Form 10-10EC, Application for Extended Care Services

1151 Claim A claim for benefits under 38 U.S.C. Section 1151 as a result of injury caused by VA treatment or rehabilitation services similar to a medical malpractice claim.

A&A   Aid and attendance

AAO   Assistant adjudication officer

ABCMR   Army Board for Correction of Military Records

ACAP Annual clothing allowance payment

ADA   Americans with Disabilities Act

ADHC Adult day health care

ADL   Activities of daily living

ADT   Active duty for training

AFB   Air Force Base

AFBCMR   Air Force Board for Correction of Military Records

AFHRA   Air Force Historical Research Agency

AFI   Air Force instruction

AFIP Armed Forces Institute of Pathology

AGG   Aggravated in service

AHRC Army Human Resources Command

AL   American Legion

ALJ   Administrative Law Judge

ALS   Amyotrophic lateral sclerosis

AMC   Appeals Management Center

AML   Acute myelogenous leukemia

AMVETS   American Veterans

AO   Agent Orange or adjudication officer

AOCAP   Agent Orange Class Assistance Program

AOJ   Agency of original jurisdiction

AOR   Agent Orange Registry

APA   Administrative Procedures Act

Appellee   The party in an appeal who is defending the decision on appeal. In the Veterans Court, the VA Secretary is always the Appellee.

Appellant   The party in an appeal who is challenging the decision on appeal. In the Veterans Court, the claimant seeking benefits (veteran or dependent) is always the Appellant.

ARBA Army Review Boards Agency

AVSCM   Assistant Veterans Service Center Manager

AWA   All Writs Act

AWOLAbsent without official leave

BCD   Bad conduct discharge

BCMR Board for Correction of Military Records

BCNR Board for Correction of Naval Records

BDD   Benefits Delivery at Discharge

BDN   Benefits Delivery Network

BHL   Bilateral hearing loss

Board The Board of Veterans' Appeals or "BVA".

BVA   The Board of Veterans' Appeals. The Board is the organization within VA that reviews initial rating decisions when the claimant files a Notice of Disagreement.

C-file Claims file. VA creates a hard copy paper file for each claimant that contains all the documents related to that claimant since the first application for benefits. C-files can contain thousands of pages of documents and must be physically shipped between offices when claims are reviewed by different VA groups or the Veterans Court.

CAAF Court of Appeals for the Armed Forces

CAVC The Unites States Court of Appeals for Veterans Claims. The appellate court to which claimants can appeal adverse Board decisions. Also known as the "Veterans Court."

C&P   Compensation and Pension

CARES   Capital Asset Realignment for Enhanced Services

CAVC Court of Appeals for Veterans Claims

CBO   Chief business office

CBOC Community Based Outpatient Clinic

CCF   Compound comminuted fracture

CDR   Counter designation of record

CFR   Code of Federal Regulations

CG   Coast Guard

CGBCMR   Coast Guard Board for Correction of Military Records

CHAMPUS   Department of Defense Civilian Health and Medical Program of the Uniformed Service

CHAMPVA   Civilian Health and Medical Program of the Department of Veterans Affairs

CHR   Consolidated health record

CIB   Combat Infantryman Badge

Claim Number   Each claimant is assigned an unique VA claim number that VA uses to identify that claimant for life. Claimants should put their claim number on each document and correspondence sent to VA.

CLC   VA Community Living Center (formerly VA Nursing Home Care Units)

CLL   Chronic lymphocytic leukemia

CMB   Combat Medical Badge

CMD   Chief Medical Director

CMO   Chief Medical Officer

CNHC Community nursing home care

CO   VA Central Office or commanding officer

COD   Character of discharge

COG   Convenience of the government

COLA Cost-of-living adjustment

Compensation A monetary benefit awarded based on the degree of disability caused by a service-connected condition.

CONUS The contiguous United States

COVA Court of Veterans Appeals (Renamed Court of Appeals for Veterans Claims)

COWC Committee on Waivers and Compromises

CPI   Claims Processing Improvement

CRC   Community residential center

CRDP Concurrent retirement and disability pay

CRSC Combat-related special compensation

CUE   Clear and unmistakable error

CURR Center for Units Records Research

CWT   VA Compensated Work Therapy Program

DAV   Disabled American Veterans

DBQ   Disability Benefits Questionnaire

DC   Diagnostic code

DD   Dishonorable discharge

DD-214   Discharge certificate

DDD   Degenerative disc disease

DEA   Dependent's educational assistance

DES   Disability evaluation system

DFAS   Defense Finance and Accounting Services

DFR   Dropped from the rolls

DIC   Death & Indemnity Compensation. A benefit awarded to surviving spouses and qualifying dependents when a service-connected condition is a cause of a veteran's death.

DM   Diabetes mellitus

DMZ   Demilitarized zone

DOD   Department of Defense

DRB   Discharge Review Board

DRO   Decision Review Officer. Usually an experienced member of a regional office rating team who reviews a rating decision at the request of the claimant after an initial denial. DRO review is optional and cannot change decisions favorable to a claimant.

DSM   American Psychiatric Association's Diagnostic and Statistical Manual for Mental Disorders

DSO   Department service officer

DTR   Deep tendon reflexes

DVA   The Department of Veterans Affairs. A technically more accurate acronym than "VA," although not as widely used.

EAD   Entry on active duty

EAJA Equal Access to Justice Act

eBenefits   VA online portal that allows veterans to manage their benefits and personal information.

ECA   Expedited Claims Adjudication Initiative

ED   Erectile dysfunction

EGC   Electrocardiogram

EKG   Electrocardiogram

EOB   Explanation of benefits

EOD   Entry on Duty or Explosive Ordinance Disposal

EVR   Eligibility verification report

FDC   Fully Developed Claim

Federal Circuit   The United States Court of Appeals for the Federal Circuit. The federal appellate court to which claimants and VA can appeal Veteran Court decisions.

FOIA Freedom of Information Act

Form 9   The VA form that must be submitted after receipt of a Statement of the Case to perfect an appeal to the Board of Veterans Appeals.

FTCA Federal Tort Claims Act

GAO Government Accounting Office

GC   General counsel

GPO Government Printing Office

GSW   Gun shot wound

GWS   Gulf war syndrome

HB   Housebound

HIPAAHealth Insurance Portability and Accountability Act

HISA   Home improvement and structural alterations

HIV   Human immunodeficiency virus

HO   Hearing officer

IED   Improvised explosive device

IG   Inspector general

IME   Independent medical expert or independent medical evaluation

INC   Incurred in service

IOM   Institute of Medicine

IOP   Internal operating procedures

IRIS   Inquiry Routing and Information System

IU   Individual unemployability

IVAP   Income for VA purposes

JAG   Judge Advocate General

JMR   Joint motion for remand

JSRRC Joint Services Records Research Center

LOD   Line of duty

LOM   Limitation of motion

LSW   Licensed social worker

M21-1MR   Adjudication Procedures Manual Rewrite

M-1   VA Healthcare Adjudication Manual

M-21   VA Claims Adjudication Manual

MACR   Missing air crew reports

MAPR   Maximum annual pension rate

MGIB   Montgomery GI Bill

MIB   Marine index bureau

MOS   Military occupational specialty

MPR   Military personnel records

MRI   Magnetic resonance imaging

MST   Military Sexual Trauma

NA   National Archives

NARA   National Archives and Record Administration

NAS   National Academy of Sciences

NAUS   National Association for Uniformed Services

NHL   Non-hodgkins lymphoma

NMCB   U.S. Navy Mobile Construction Battalion

NOA   Notice of Appeal

NOD   Notice of Disagreement. Claimants must file a written NOD within one year of receiving a rating decision to be able to appeal that decision.

NOS   Not otherwise specified

NPC   Naval Personnel Command

NPRC   National Personnel Records Center

NRPC   Naval Reserve Personnel Command

NSC   Non-service-connected

NSLI   National Service Life Insurance

NSO   National service officer

NVLSP   National Veterans Legal Services Program

OEF   Operation Enduring Freedom

OGC   Office of the General Counsel

OIF   Operation Iraqi Freedom

OIG   Office of Inspector General

OMPF Official military personnel file

OPC   Outpatient clinic

OPT   Outpatient treatment

OQP   Office of Quality and Performance

OTH   Other than honorable

PDBR Physical Disability Board of Review

PDR   Physicians' Desk Reference

PEB   Physical Evaluation Board

Pension A VA benefit based on financial need available to fully disabled veterans who served during a time of war.

PERMS Permanent Electronic Records Management System

PG   Persian Gulf

PGW Persian Gulf War

PIES Personnel Information Exchange System

PIF   Pending issue file

PMC Pension Maintenance Center

POA Power of attorney

POW Prisoner-of-war

PRC Polytrauma Rehabilitation Center

Presumption A legal term meaning that no evidence of a nexus between a current medical condition and an in-service occurrence is required. A claimant currently suffer from a "presumptive condition" only needs to establish he or she experienced the specified in-service event to be awarded service connection. See related Knowledge Book.

PT   Physical therapy or permanent total disability

PTE   Peace time era

PTSD   Posttraumatic stress disorder

PEBLO Physical Evaluation Board Liaison Officer

RAD   Release from active duty

Rating Decision   The initial VA decision on a claim which either grants or denies an award or "continues" the claim for further development.

Rating Schedule   The table of medical conditions and disabilities established by law that VA raters use to determine the degree of disability for compensation purposes.

Remand Return of a decision to the organization that made it for additional review and revision. The Board remands rating decisions to the originating regional office. The Veterans Court Remands Board decisions back to the Board.

RMC   Records Management Center

RMO   Records Management Officer

RN   Registered nurse

RO   Regional Office

ROTC Reserve Officers' Training Corps

RVN   Republic of Vietnam

RVSR Rating Veterans Service Representative

SBP   Survivor Benefit Plan

SC   Service-connected

SDRP Special Discharge Review Program

SDVI Service Disabled Veterans' Insurance

Secretary   The Secretary of Veterans Affairs. The Cabinet officer who is the administrative head of VA.

Service Connection   A requirement that a claimant for VA compensation must (1) have a current medical condition; (2) identify an event or condition during military service; and (3) establish a nexus or connection between the medical condition and the in-service event or condition. Without establishing service connection, VA will not award compensation benefits.

SF   Special forces

SGLI Servicemembers' Group Life Insurance

SMC Special Monthly Compensation. Additional compensation available to the most seriously disabled veterans for anatomical loss of limbs or loss of use of body parts, aid and attendance, and other special needs.

SMP Special monthly pension

SMR Service medical record

SN   Service number

SOC   Statement of the Case. A document that VA must prepare and provide to a claimant who has submitted a timely Notice of Disagreement. The purpose of an SOC is to identify the facts and law VA used to reach the decision(s) with which the claimant disagrees.

SPD   Separation program designator

SPN   Separation program number

SRD   Schedule for Rating Disabilities

SSA   Social Security Administration

SSB   Special separation benefits

SSDI Social Security Disability Income

SSI   Supplemental Security Income

SSN   Social Security Number

SSOC   Supplemental Statement of the Case

STR   Service treatment records

STS   Soft tissue sarcoma

TAD   Temporary active duty

TBI   Traumatic brain injury

TCDD   2,3,7,8-tetrachlorodibenzodioxin

TDIU   Total Disability based on Individual Unemployability. A special rating that considers whether a claimant who does not meet the rating schedule requirements for 100% disability is still unable to work in a substantially gainful occupation. A TDIU award pays benefits at the 100% scheduler rate even though the actual rating percentage is less than 100%.

TRDL   Temporary disabled retirement list

TDY   Temporary duty

UCMJ   Uniform Code of Military Justice

U.S.C. United States Code

U.S.C.A.   United States Code Annotated

U.S.C.S.   United States Code Service

USGLI   United States Government Life Insurance

USJSRRC   United States Joint Service Records Research Center

VA   The most commonly used acronym for the Department of Veterans Affairs.

VACO   VA Central Office

VAF   VA form

VAGC   VA General Counsel

VAHAC   VA Health Administration Center

VAMC VA Medical Center

VAOGC   VA Office of the General Counsel

VAOIG   VA Office of the Inspector General

VAOPC   VA outpatient clinic

VAR   VA regulation

VARO VA Regional Office

VBA   Veterans Benefits Administration

VCAA Veterans Claims Assistance Act

VEAP Post-Vietnam Era Veterans' Educational Assistance Program

Veterans Court   Another common name for the United States Court of Appeals for Veterans Claims. See also CAVC.

VFW   Veterans of Foreign Wars

VGLI   Veterans' Group Life Insurance

VHA   Veterans Health Administration

VISN   Veterans Integrated Service Network

VJRA Veterans Judicial Review Act

VLJ   Veterans Law Judge. A member of the Board of Veterans' Appeals who hears appeals from claimants who disagree with a rating decision.

VMLI Veterans' Mortgage Life Insurance

VONAPP   Veterans Online Application. A VA website for electronically applying for VA benefits. https://www.ebenefits.va.gov/ebenefits-portal/ebenefits.portal?_nfpb=true&_nfxr=false&_pageLabel=Vonapp

VRC   Vocational rehabilitation counseling

VSCM Veterans Service Center Manager

VSM   Vietnam Service Medal

VSO   Veterans service organization

VSR   Veterans Service Representative

WRIISC   War Related Illness and Injury Center

REFERENCE MATERIAL

Thousand of reference material to include Title 38 CFR Part 3, Title 38 CFR Part 4, Adjudication Manual M21-1 and other useful tables, statistics, studies, addenda.

Made in the USA
Columbia, SC
17 October 2023

24244590R00048